STILLNESS, INSIGHT, AND EMPTINESS

Also by Lama Dudjom Dorjee

Falling Off the Roof of the World
Heartfelt Advice

Stillness, Insight, and Emptiness

Buddhist Meditation from the Ground Up

Lama Dudjom Dorjee

SNOW LION

BOSTON & LONDON

2013

Snow Lion
An imprint of Shambhala Publications, Inc.
Horticultural Hall
300 Massachusetts Avenue
Boston, Massachusetts 02115
www.shambhala.com

Drawing on page 48 by Robert Beer, from *The Encyclopedia of Tibetan
Symbols and Motifs,* by Robert Beer, © 1999. Reprinted by arrangement
with Shambhala Publications, Inc. www.shambhala.com.

9 8 7 6 5 4 3 2 1

First Edition
Printed in the United States of America

♾ This edition is printed on acid-free paper that meets the
American National Standards Institute z39.48 Standard.
♻ Shambhala makes every effort to print on recycled paper.
For more information please visit www.shambhala.com.

Distributed in the United States by Random House, Inc.,
and in Canada by Random House of Canada Ltd

Designed by Gopa & Ted2, Inc.

Library of Congress Cataloging-in-Publication Data

Dudjom Dorjee, Lama.
Stillness, insight, and emptiness: Buddhist meditation from
the ground up / Lama Dudjom Dorjee.—First Edition.
pages cm
ISBN 978-1-55939-420-8 (pbk.)
1. Meditation—Buddhism. I. Title.
BQ5612.D83 2013
294.3'4435—dc23
2013002684

Contents

Foreword:
A Letter from His Eminence Tai Situ Rinpoche

As requested, I am imparting a few words on behalf of Lama D. Dorjee's latest publication, *Stillness, Insight, and Emptiness: Buddhist Meditation from the Ground Up*.

This is the third Dharma book written by Lama D. Dorjee, conveying a profound teaching in a concise and simple style. As a guide to students of meditation at all levels, this book will benefit those seeking to understand and practice the Buddha's holy Dharma.

May excellent virtue increase,

The Twelfth Kenting Tai Situpa
September 1, 2011

MY PRAYER AND ASPIRATION

Please feel free to recite this prayer, either silently or aloud, just as if you were reciting it along with me. You can do this any time you like, but especially each time you begin reading this book.

To the three jewels—the Buddha, the Dharma, and the Sangha—

To the three roots—the Lamas, Yidams, and Dharma Protectors—

To all you sources of refuge: consider your vows to help all sentient beings forever end their suffering, break the chains of samsara, and find true freedom in the path of liberation.

Buddhas and bodhisattvas, please grant your blessings that our aspirations and prayers may be fulfilled.

Through the negative thoughts and unvirtuous actions of beings in these degenerate times, and the turmoil of the outer and inner imbalance of the four elements, we are beset by a horde of human and animal diseases, both old and new.

Buddhas and bodhisattvas, please grant your blessings that our aspirations and prayers may be fulfilled.

Everywhere on the earth, nagas, gyalpos, and maras bring suffering. We see these manifest as blight, drought, and famine. They reveal themselves as terrible storms such as hurricanes, floods, and tornadoes. We even see their presence in the form of weapons of mass destruction, nuclear, chemical, and biological. Even the four elements are angry. We see their distress at their state of imbalance as earthquakes, volcanoes, and wildfires.

Buddhas and bodhisattvas, please grant your blessings that our aspirations and prayers may be fulfilled.

We hang at the very edge of the precipice of environmental catastrophe. Human activity has brought this planet to the brink of destruction. The air we breathe and the water we drink have become toxic to our systems. The atmosphere no longer provides us the necessary protection from the sun's powerful rays. Every year, more and more species disappear from the planet, never to be seen again.

Buddhas and bodhisattvas, please grant your blessings that our aspirations and prayers may be fulfilled.

In particular, we are constantly threatened by the accumulation of negative thoughts and energies brought into the world by each and every individual mind. What starts as individual negativity is compounded when added to that of the rest of the world, allowing it to grow to planetary proportions. What starts as individual negativity that may result in suffering on a smaller, more personal scale as one person does physical harm to or murders another, eventually grows and spreads like a cancer. One person's negativity is added to the next person's until the world is a place of terrible invasions, wars, and genocides.

Buddhas and bodhisattvas, please grant your blessings that our aspirations and prayers be fulfilled:

That thoughts and feelings of loving-kindness and compassion increase, person-to-person and family-to-family, so that they may become nation-to-nation. Fighting and wars must be quickly pacified and eradicated; all destructive activity swiftly brought to an end.

Buddhas and bodhisattvas, please grant your blessings that our aspirations and prayers may be fulfilled:

That all beings, humans and nonhumans, naturally generate precious bodhichitta, like a mother's love for her child, but toward all sentient beings without exception. May they be free from pain and suffering of malevolent thoughts and actions.

Buddhas and bodhisattvas, please grant your blessings that our aspirations and prayers may be fulfilled:

That every corner of this planet's habitat and its every inhabitant experience true harmony and well-being. May the earth and those who live upon it find healing as disease subsides and the four elements find balance and harmony.

Buddhas and bodhisattvas, please grant your blessings that our aspirations and prayers may be fulfilled:

May all living beings be filled with joy and find freedom from fear. May their prosperity and abundance of wealth increase, unrivaled by any other time in history.

Buddhas and bodhisattvas, please grant your blessings that our aspirations and prayers may be fulfilled:

That your activities flourish and remain forever, in order to liberate all living beings from the ocean of samsara. May the doctrines of the buddha dharma spread and shine all over this universe.

Buddhas and bodhisattvas, please grant your blessings that our aspirations and prayers may be fulfilled:

That the roots of virtue spread through the soils of samsara and nirvana. By the power of our pure benevolence, may our prayers be answered; may all be accomplished in accordance with the genuine teachings of Lord Buddha.

Buddhas and bodhisattvas, please grant your blessings that our aspirations and prayers may be fulfilled.

Stillness, Insight, and Emptiness

INTRODUCTION

B REATH MEDITATION is one of the most common practices for many traditions, religious and nonreligious, Buddhist and non-Buddhist. Breathing exercises bring benefit to us at the mundane level, improving relaxation by reducing stress and anxiety, while also deepening our ability to focus our concentration. This results in general improvements to our health and sense of well-being, and to our productivity and effectiveness in all areas of our lives.

More importantly, combining breathing practices with meditation and prayer also brings great benefit on the spiritual level. We can combine simple breathing exercises with focusing the mind one-pointedly on the breath, attaching specific visualizations to the movements of our breath, or even including altruistic thoughts of others and our wishes for their happiness and well-being. When we do this, our simple breathing exercises that produce a pleasant physiological or psychological effect become something much more powerful. These breathing exercises then become spiritual meditation practices that have the power to transform the fundamental nature of the heart and mind of the practitioner and her experience of reality.

It is very important for us to recognize both the value and the profundity of the breathing practices available to us. We must remember how essential the breath is; as living beings, we are breathing all the time. Breath is a fundamental sign of life, one that all living beings have in common. The majority of sentient beings are completely unaware of their own breath until something interferes with it. When humans are in danger of suffocation, drowning, or strangulation, they become intensely aware of their very intimate relationship with their breath. However, there are even times when the breath is ragged or strained due to physical exertion or illness, and yet we are still unaware that we are breathing. As practitioners of the Buddhist techniques of breath meditation, we become not only more aware of the existence of our breath but more mindful and aware of its qualities, such as its regularity and depth. Thus, we develop an appreciation for the existence and persistence of our own breath.

Using the breath as the object of focus for our mind's attention during meditation has many benefits. First, meditating on the breath brings our focus, and thus our energy, back to the root: our body. In this lifetime, as human beings, our minds are rooted in and supported by our physical bodies. It is our body that provides our mind with a feeling of being grounded and stable. The breath is the fundamental action of the body. Without breathing, most of us cannot survive more than a few minutes. Whether we are calm or agitated, the state of our mind shows itself in the quality of our breath. When we focus our mind's attention on this action of the breath, we turn our attention away from the external world and toward the most fundamental sign of life that our body provides. As our attention turns inward, the energy that we normally put into attempting to analyze and manipulate our experience of the external world also turns inward. Thus, turning our attention inward brings the mind back home, where it can find rest and rejuvenation. From this internal experience of rest spring profound feelings of tranquility and peace.

Second, the breath is always present and requires no maintenance. If we meditate on a stone, or candle flame, or even the images in a thangka painting, we must remember to keep these things with us. We must first acquire these meditation objects, which takes effort and perhaps money. We must then carry these things with us if we think we may have a chance to meditate. We must also make certain that we do not lose them or lend them to someone else along the way. Additionally, external objects of focus often require preparation. For instance, it takes time and effort to light a candle, hang a thangka painting, or set up a shrine, regardless of how simple or elaborate. The breath, however, does not need to be acquired; we received it on the day we were born and will continue to possess it until we leave this body. It is always with us; it cannot be lost or forgotten, lent to anyone, or stolen. The breath never requires time or energy to prepare for meditation; it is there and ready for our attention the moment we are ready to practice. When we focus on the breath, we become highly aware of the fact that the breath has its own natural richness. There is nothing that needs to be added or taken away, no improvements that need to be made. The breath only needs to be observed, and we can immediately recognize some degree of fullness of presence. Over time, this peaceful rhythm leads us easily into the state of tranquility and calm abiding that is shamatha meditation.

It is important for us to have some cultural perspective with regard to meditation, especially breath meditation. There is no word in the English language that completely and accurately describes what the Eastern traditions advocate as dharma practice. The English word *meditation* falls far short of defining the indescribable breadth and depth of the Eastern practices that we have labeled as simply "meditation." The English word *meditation* has always implied a certain amount of cogitation. For instance, Catholic monks read some scripture or devotional tract and then stop and sit in silence as they ponder the deeper and subtler meanings of that reading. One can walk into the self-help section of a bookstore and pick up any number of books that claim to contain "daily meditations." These are basically thoughts for the day that one can ponder and attempt to digest in a way that allows them to sink deeper into one's consciousness in the hope that they will then guide one's thoughts and actions in a predictably desirable way. There is nothing wrong with this at all; in fact, certain practices similar to this from the Eastern traditions have been labeled "contemplative meditation." However, this English notion of "meditation," as it is associated with contemplation, is only one tiny corner of the vast tradition of Eastern dharma practice. By the end of this book, we hope that readers will have a better understanding of meditation within the framework of shamatha, which is still only one small but significant piece of the vast scope of dharma practice.

The other Western idea of meditation that one hears described, especially by those who have never meditated, is to simply "clear one's mind." While this is a great trick if you can do it, for most beginning meditators it's simply unattainable. As soon as one attempts to clear the mind of all current thoughts, a new flood of thoughts develops to fill the empty space. Many in the West think that the goal of meditation is to not have thoughts, or even emotions, at all, and for the mind to remain empty for whatever amount of time the meditator wishes to practice. The nature of mind itself is that thoughts continuously arise and dissipate. To have no thoughts would be to have no mind. However, our ability to choose what we do with those thoughts is what characterizes our skill as meditators. One Eastern definition of meditation is to be able to focus the mind on a single object for the duration of twelve or more breaths. This comes closer to describing what we will discuss in this book as shamatha, or breath meditation.

Another cultural phenomenon that most Westerners experience early in their practice is sleepiness. In the U.S. in particular, we are very used to waking up, getting caffeinated, and go, go, going all day long. Even when we rest and "relax," we do so while engaged in some sort of activity such as sitting in front of the television or computer and continuing to busy our mind with attempts to digest ever more sensory input, input that is typically of questionable quality. Generally speaking, the only time we ever stop doing and consuming and allow ourselves to be still and rest for a moment is when we lie down to go to sleep. Several implications from this lifestyle can be drawn, two of which we should emphasize here. One, because we are not still, quiet, and focused very often (if ever), we aren't very good at it. Two, if we are good at it, it only tends to result in one thing: going to sleep. So this is how we've trained our minds.

We very rarely just sit in quiet solitude and enjoy being present in the moment. Instead, any time we try to relax, we practically pass out, because our bodies and minds believe that relaxation should always translate directly into sleep. Thus, for many of us, as soon as we begin to enjoy the benefit of meditation that is slowing down the barrage of thoughts through our mind, and feeling our body unwind from its worldly tension, we immediately begin struggling with a new obstacle: sleepiness.

Unfortunately, this American way of living is spreading everywhere in the world, even in the East. Go to Beijing or Tokyo and you won't find many meditators on the busy streets of those or other major cities. The good news is this: the body and mind can be retrained. Over time, as one continues to attempt bringing the mind into a state of tranquility and calm abiding while maintaining a sense of transcendent awareness and luminous clarity, that sleepiness will vanish. In fact, it has been shown that meditators tend to get a much higher quality of sleep than nonpractitioners. This means that when meditators are awake they are also more alert, and someone who is well rested is far less likely to feel groggy or dull when relaxing into a deeper meditative state.

The mind's habitual state, the activity to which we are most accustomed, is a mind that jumps from one object of attention to the next like an excited monkey. Therefore, if we want to change the state of our mind from one of distraction and agitation, we must simply change its habits. We must get out of the habit of distraction and into the habit of concentration. It is important to understand that the mind requires rigorous discipline and training, using breath meditation to change its habit so that its natural state is revealed as one of peace and tranquility. We have cultivated our habit of distraction over the course of not only this lifetime but potentially many lifetimes. The fact that any of the great sages ever cultivated a state of mind that is focused and free from distraction shows just how powerful meditation can be. All great beings, the buddhas and bodhisattvas, started out as ordinary practitioners like us. They too were distracted and agitated, and yet, through the practice of meditation, they quickly overcame the patterns and habits of distraction.

The great beings of the Buddhist tradition all defeated their own distractions and cultivated the transcendent awareness that is the awakened mind through the practice of breath meditation called shamatha. When practiced with diligence and determination, shamatha will inevitably lead us also toward tranquility and liberation from suffering.

༄༅། །ཚུལ་བརྟགས་པ་ཕྱིར་ལྷུམ་བ་བ་སྒྲུབ་མཛད་གནས།

།།ལྷ།།གཀགརྒྱགས་ལྤྱལ་ཏ་གམཚོ་བ་པ་ཏ་ལྷུ་བ།

གནི་པ་བ་ཕྱལ་ཏ་ཀྲུ་ལ་པ་པུ་རྒྱག་པ་པ་ཏ་ལྷ་ལྤ།།

གཔུལ་བ་ཀྲུ་ཀ་རྩུལ་པ་ཏ་ལྷ་ལྤ།།

བཞི་བ་ཀྲུ་ཆེ་ལ་བ་རྒུ་པ་ཏ་ལྷ་ལྤ།།

དྲུ་བ་རྒྱལ་པུ།།ཀྲུ་ཏ་ལྷ་ལྤ།།

།ཀ་བ་ར་བ་ཀྲུ་ཏ་ལྷ་ལྤ།།

བ།ག་བ།།ཀཀ་བ་ཤྲུ་པ་ཏ་ལྷ་ལྤ།།

བཀྲུ་བ་པ་ཀྲུ་པ་པ་ཏ་ལྷ་ལྤ།།

།གུ་བ་ཆེ་བ་ཏཞ་ར་བ་སྐྱ་ར་བ་ཏ་ལྷ་ལྤ།།

བཀྲུ་བ་ཅ།།བ་ལ་བ་ཏ་ལྷ་ལྤ།།

བཀྲུ་གཞ་གཆེ་གཆ་བ་ཀ་ཕྱལ་བ་ཤྲུ་པ་ཏ་ལྷ་ལྤ།།

བཀྲུ་གཞི་བ་ཀྲུ་ལྤྱ་།།ཀྲུ་ལ་བ་ཀ་པ་པ་ཏ་ལྷ་ལྤ།།

THE TWELVE DEEDS OF SHAKYAMUNI BUDDHA.
CALLIGRAPHY BY LAMA DUDJOM DORJEE.

1. The Twelve Deeds of Shakyamuni Buddha

All of the teachings in this book must begin with Lord Shakyamuni Buddha. It was through his remarkable actions that he showed that we humans, born from a womb just as he was, can also attain enlightenment by emulating the lessons of his life.

1. The Buddha's Birth

The Buddha's first deed was to descend to our world as a bodhisattva from a buddha-field known as Tushita. He particularly chose the human realm within which to take his form. He specifically chose the Shakya clan as the best family into which to be born, for this would provide him the best circumstances from which to benefit sentient beings.

2. The Buddha's Parents

His father was King Shuddhodana, one of the most powerful and influential kings of his time. His mother was Queen Maya Devi. She was not only beautiful but also remarkably wise. Queen Maya Devi dreamed that an unusual white elephant entered her body through her side, so she knew to expect an extraordinary child.

3. The Buddha's Birthplace

Their child was born in a northern Indian region within view of the Himalayas, in what is now called Nepal. He was born while his mother was on her way to her own mother's home where she intended to give birth, as was the custom. The baby emerged from his mother's body as she held on to tree branches in the Lumbini flower garden, where the gods Indra and Brahma prophesied that the child belonged to the lineage of enlightened beings, the buddhas. His parents named him Siddhartha.

Immediately after birth, he was able to take seven steps, and lotuses sprang forth from his footprints. He could also speak, saying as he pointed up and then down, "In the worlds above or the worlds below, there is no one like me. I am supreme beyond all beings in the human realm. My wisdom is immutable and unequaled among humans; I am Buddha; I am fully awake."

4. The Buddha's Childhood

As a youth, Siddhartha was instructed in and mastered all the arts of war. Through contests of skill, he won the hand of the beautiful princess Gopa. These contests included competitions of strength in various sports: riding, archery, and lifting weights. In tests of knowledge of worldly topics he was infallible and far beyond the skill or concept of ordinary beings. He was invincible in all contests.

5. The Buddha's Worldly Skills

Siddhartha was also skilled in other worldly ways. He was a devoted son and performed the usual royal duties. These ranged from the judging of disputes among subjects to courting and entertaining the ladies. In essence, he fully experienced his own humanity and demonstrated his excellence in the realm of worldly pursuits.

6. The Buddha Renounces Worldly Life

From the time of his birth, Siddhartha's parents sheltered him from the sufferings of human life. Eventually it came to pass that Siddhartha wandered outside of the controlled environment of the palace area. There he saw a person disabled by advanced age, a person suffering from a serious illness, and a corpse being carried to the cremation grounds followed by a group of weeping mourners. Siddhartha realized that his parents had deceived him about the pain and suffering of human existence and became determined to discover the truth. Later, Siddhartha noticed a poor wanderer in simple cotton garb who seemed peaceful and happy in the midst of the city's chaos. After he saw the suffering of this realm, he wanted to discover the antidote to human suffering. He decided to leave home and renounce worldly life. When his father tried to discourage him, Siddhartha asked if his parent could guarantee that he would never die or ever fall ill, that he would stay young and never become poor. With that, Siddhartha left the palace in the middle of the night, leaving his sleeping wife and new son.

7. THE BUDDHA BECOMES AN ASCETIC

Siddhartha vowed to follow the ascetic tradition until he found an ultimate solution to the sufferings of samsara. As a sign of renunciation, he removed his headdress and cut off his royal topknot. This is the initial preparation for becoming an ascetic, a monk. He set off to find a tranquil spot in which to work on the problem of the human condition.

8. THE BUDDHA ATTAINS ENLIGHTENMENT

Following the sadhu tradition with other spiritual companions, he renounced all worldly attachments to sensory objects. Hoping to discover the antidote to overcome the sufferings of human birth, he fasted so long that he resembled a skeleton and was nearing the end of his life. One day, he was bathing in a stream when a village girl named Sujata passed by. Seeing how emaciated he was, she offered him a bowl of sweet creamed rice. This first meal not only restored his health and energy, but also brought him to a moment of profound realization of the human experience of reality. He saw that extreme asceticism was no more the answer than was the extreme luxury of life in the palace. He decided that the middle way was the best course of action, not following the extremes. Because he indulged his own hunger, his human need for sustenance, his ascetic companions denigrated and abandoned him. He looked for a place where he could sit in meditation as he explored this middle path as the antidote to suffering. Siddhartha found a bodhi tree where he made the vow not to stir from beneath that tree until he had discovered the means within this Middle Path to permanently alleviate all suffering. Then he went into a deeply concentrated form of meditation.

Early dawn came. With crossed legs, he never moved, indestructible as a vajra. He did not wake from deep samadhi until the crucial moment arrived. The very Earth was called to testify to Siddhartha's worthiness. It was at that moment that his enlightenment occurred. According to the sutras, at the moment of his awakening, he radiated an aura of light. Flowers rained from the heavens, and other wondrous manifestations occurred.

After his awakening, he later reported these thoughts:

> My realization was so very profound that I was unsure how to ever communicate that to my fellow human beings. Imagine this realization being like amrita—the nectar of the gods. It was so delicious, beyond anything tasted, touched, smelled, sensed, or thought. Something that could grant immortality and even bring one back from death's door. How could I ever tell anyone about this? Should I even try? Maybe I should just go and meditate in the forest away from everyone.

And so he sat silently in a perfectly balanced state of awareness for seven days, until the gods Indra and Brahma intervened. They begged him to teach others, to "turn the wheel of dharma" for the sake of other beings.

Now Siddhartha truly became the Buddha. A buddha is one who is awakened, one who knows everything, whose mind is complete knowingness. The state of complete knowing, of being fully awake, is experienced only by a buddha.

9. The Buddha Turns the Wheel of Dharma

At last, he got up and walked to Rishipatan Sarnath to find his five former ascetic companions. Then, at what is now Sarnath, near Varanasi, he delivered his first sermon, which is described as the first turning of the wheel of the dharma. After hearing his first discourse, each of his five former companions received spiritual realizations. They then offered him their bowls, in tribute to his achievement. In their ascetic lives, their bowls were their only possessions.

10. The Buddha Conquers the Maras

Buddha was attacked by inner and outer conflicts with the appearance of Mara. Typically characterized as a demon or malevolent spirit but symbolic of the negative forces that arise as obstacles on the path to enlightenment, Mara is often described as being four in number: First, there is the Mara of Karma. This is the demon of the aggregates, the five skandhas, which form the foundation for suffering within the realm of samsara. Second, there is the Mara of Afflictive Emotions, the demon that provokes suffering. Third is the Mara of Death. This demon is not only the suffering of the end of a life but also death in the sense that all phenomena are momentary, transient, or impermanent, which is a cause of so many of our sufferings. The fourth demon is translated as the Child of the Gods, which is the demon that symbolizes not only our tendencies of mental wandering but also our attachment to the phenomena we apprehend and perceive as truly existent. At this stage of the Buddha's path, because he had attained self-mastery, these maras were incapable of disrupting his state of being perfectly established in complete awakening, liberated from all suffering, fully enlightened.

11. The Buddha Performs Miracles

Buddha performed many miracles. At one point the King of Serpents, a multiheaded cobra, spread his several hoods to act as an elaborate umbrella to shelter Buddha from rain and sun while he sat deep in absorption. His adversary Mara reappeared to him and tried to tempt him back to a worldly life of influence and power. Mara manifested beautiful and seductive offspring in an attempt to seduce Buddha to return to a life of indulgence in sensory pleasures. However, Buddha was unshakable in the face of all the attempts of Mara.

12. The Buddha's Death

Finally, the last deed of the Buddha was his achievement of Mahaparinirvana. At that time, he left behind 84,000 different methods and means by which we too can escape the sufferings of our own bondage within the cycle of existence that is samsara.

The Buddha entered parinirvana at around the age of eighty, during the time of a full moon. It was in a grove of mango trees, near the city of Kushinagar, that he asked his close disciples to set up a couch for him. There, lying on his right side, facing west, his head supported by his hand, he clearly knew that death was approaching.

The Buddha's last words are reputed to be,

All things which are made of parts eventually come apart.
All exhaustible phenomena contain suffering and dissatisfaction.

All phenomena are empty of inherent existence.
Be mindful and achieve the awakened state! Nirvana is peace.

Toward midnight, having experienced all levels of meditation in sequence, he left all existence. His transition could have been to transform his body into crystal light and rainbows, but he chose instead to leave his body behind, so that his students could witness the inevitability of death and thereby encourage their practice.

This is the mantra that evokes Shakyamuni Buddha:

OM MUNI MUNI MAHA MUNI YE SWA HA!

SHAKYAMUNI BUDDHA.

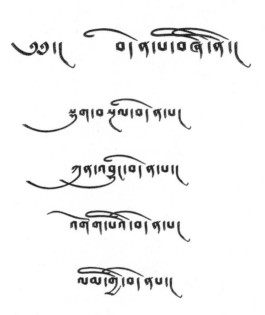

THE FOUR NOBLE TRUTHS.
CALLIGRAPHY BY LAMA DUDJOM DORJEE.

2. The Four Noble Truths

THE TEACHINGS of Shakyamuni Buddha are categorized into three groups. These are called the three turnings of the wheel of dharma. It is from the three turnings that the three main types of Buddhism originated; these traditions are referred to as the three vehicles. The first turning of the wheel of dharma is generally summed up by the four noble truths and the commentaries surrounding them.

It is from the first turning that the earliest schools of Buddhism derive their fundamental guiding philosophies and practices of personal liberation. It was this emphasis upon self-redemption which led later schools of Buddhism to pejoratively refer to the earlier tradition as the Hinayana, the "lesser" vehicle. In the second turning of the wheel of dharma, the seeds were sown for the Mahayana tradition with its subtle philosophies and active practices of compassion. In Mahayana, which means "greater vehicle," the mission of liberation has been broadened as being for the benefit of all sentient beings. In the third turning of the wheel of dharma, the Buddha gave teachings that lead to the most rapid path to liberation, encapsulated by the Vajrayana or Mantrayana tradition.

There is sometimes a mistake made in the way that students perceive the three turnings and the subsequent three traditions that spring from those three sets of teachings. Students tend to assume that they should simply choose which of the three turnings most appeals to them and then study those teachings and apply those practices.

Unfortunately, the second assumption that quickly follows is that the first turning and its practices are lower, lesser, and for those with poor faculties for study and practice. Therefore, the second turning is then considered intermediate and the third advanced and by far the superior. The conclusion is quickly drawn that the student should have nothing to do with the first two sets of teachings and skip immediately to the third, thereby fast-tracking his path to enlightenment. However, this view does not serve the potential dharma student very well at all.

The view that is most correct and that will best provide for the student's education and practice is a view of personal liberation as the essential foundation that must be laid if any further progress is to be made using teachings from either of the other two vehicles.

Attempting to make progress within the Mahayana or Vajrayana vehicles without study, contemplation, and practice within the framework of the first turning is like trying to build the walls and roof of a house without first creating some sort of foundation for the rest of that house to stand on: the walls and roof will stand and protect us from the elements only at first.

Over time, the ground below can move, hard wind and rains will come, and eventually shifts will occur that will cause the entire house to collapse. A properly built house always begins with a foundation. The ground must be leveled, and, if it is not firm, a foundation must be created from rocks or concrete. Students should be encouraged to view the so-called Hinayana as a foundation made of indestructible materials. When the foundation is strong, it can withstand the challenges that come during practice of the other two yanas.

No matter how storms might damage the roof and walls, so long as the foundation remains intact, repair and rebuilding can always be done. As we have already stated, the earliest schools are based on the first turning of the wheel of dharma. This first set of the Buddha's teachings is known as the four noble truths, which are as follows:

1. The truth of suffering
2. The truth of the cause of suffering
3. The truth of the cessation of suffering
4. The truth of the path out of suffering

When students study, contemplate, and meditate on the four noble truths, they reach a point of profound realization and a depth of certainty that creates the indestructible foundation upon which all other aspects of their practice are built.

1. The Truth of Suffering

Although most sentient beings are unaware of it from moment to moment, they are almost always mired in suffering of some form or another. There are sufferings related to material wealth, physical health, and psychological and emotional fluctuations. In fact, many of the things that we believe are sources of happiness for us actually only serve to perpetuate our suffering.

The most obvious example of suffering in the human realm is that of physical suffering. Many people are sick, disfigured, maimed, and in pain. It is easy for us to see these types of suffering and say to ourselves, "I am lucky! I don't have any of those types of suffering!" However, as human beings we all suffer the experiences of birth, old age, sickness, and death. We may not be dealing with the direct experience of suffering that those four occasions inspire every day of our lives. However, we spend a significant amount of time living in fear of experiences of physical suffering.

We spend even more time and energy either entertaining suffering or attempting to avoid it. Entertaining suffering means that we give physical suffering time and energy. We can do this by attempting to recuperate from sickness, going to the doctor, resting, taking medicine, helping a sick person who is near or dear to us to get well, dealing with that person's death, etc. Also, we can spend much time in the gym, or spend money on preventative measures and even plastic surgery to try to slow down or stop sickness, old age, and death.

There is great suffering in relation to material wants and needs. Again, it is easy to look at the poorest people in the world and see their suffering as they starve to death or suffer from exposure to the elements because they have no shelter. We see this and feel as though we are not suffering because we, unlike them, have the basic necessities of life. However, even when we have our necessities met, we then suffer from the fear that we might lose those most basic means of survival. Also, we may suffer from desire because we want more exquisite and luxurious things, whether they are needed or not. This type of suffering is limitless because no matter how much we have, the craving for more never ceases.

The more we have, the more habitual the craving becomes, so that we become even more desirous the more we accumulate. This type of suffering becomes even worse because the more we wish to accumulate, the more we fear losing what we have already accumulated. This particular cycle of suffering is easily recognized in many of the richest yet most unhappy people in the world today.

Traditionally, all suffering fits into one of three categories. First, there is what is referred to as *the suffering of suffering itself,* which is what we experience when our mind encounters anything that it would prefer to avoid as well as those sufferings that no one has ever escaped: birth, sickness, old age, and death. Second, there is the *suffering of change,* which is what we endure any time we experience loss or even the fear of loss of something to which we are attached. Third, there are the *inherent sufferings,* which refer to the basic dissatisfaction pervading all forms of life because of conditioned states, the five skandhas which underlie our clinging and form our future sufferings.

It is important for us to recognize that on its face this type of worldview, one that accepts that we are surrounded by suffering every moment of our lives, seems dark and depressing. However, just because it poses us difficulty in the form of a very uncomfortable truth does not make it any less valid. In fact, how would it be possible for us to ever find a solution to this kind of problem if we weren't aware that it existed? So, although unpleasant at first, when we realize the truth of this view, and even use our intense conviction in that truth to fuel our practice of buddha dharma, then what seems like a negative view is actually quite useful to us, and therefore a reason to rejoice that we have found the dharma.

In most instances, upon hearing this truth explained, students with even the slightest intellectual faculties are quick to concede the logic of this worldview as though it were obvious. However, when they leave a teaching on this first noble truth they immediately resume a life of grasping, attachment, aversion, and all the sufferings that stem from such life choices. Mere mundane knowledge is not the deep conviction necessary to slow our habitual momentum enough to change course and embark on a path away from suffering and toward liberation.

We must have a certainty in the first noble truth that causes us to place dharma practice above all other priorities. The ancient texts say that "We must practice as if our hair is on fire." This may seem odd, but if we see the inevitability of particular outcomes from continuing our mundane approaches to finding happiness, it begins to make more sense. Because of the certainty of the sufferings inherent in samsara, and also the certainty of our own eventual death, we should view our current situation as though our hair were literally on fire and that the only way to put the fire out is to practice dharma. This should give us an idea of the degree of urgency with which we should practice.

This sense of urgency is fine for us to talk about and it may give us an idea of how important dharma practice is. It may even give us the desire to have this kind of urgency. Unfortunately, many of us are addicted to samsara more surely than the worst alcoholic or drug addict is bound to their habit: we may understand that our addiction is the cause of all of our problems; we may understand that the solution is to remove the source of the addiction from our lives; but that does not mean that we actually *want* to give up our addiction. It is therefore quite unlikely that we will succeed in removing the addiction. Worst of all, it is almost impossible that we will one day conquer the very root of the addiction itself. Fortunately, dharma practice possesses that very possibility.

To dig out the very root of our attachment to the pleasures of samsara, we must practice contemplative meditation. We can begin by simply sitting on our meditation cushion and thinking of all the things that have caused us suffering in the past or even present. In this way we contemplate the suffering of suffering itself. We can also sit and contemplate all of the things that we have been attached to and then lost, or those things that we possessed and enjoyed only to find that they required maintenance or other costs that caused us suffering. In this way we contemplate the suffering of change.

We should also sometimes sit and try to think of all the times that we and others have suffered as a result of birth, old age, sickness, and death. In the same way, we should sit and try to think of anyone we know who has managed to completely escape those four sufferings. It is in this way that we contemplate the inherent sufferings. During these sessions of contemplative meditation on the first noble truth, we must not allow ourselves to become dark or depressed by our growing certainty in the inescapable and inevitable nature of suffering in the realm of samsara.

Rather, we should rejoice in the realization that we are finally seeing clearly enough to see our problems for what they really are. Without a clear understanding of our problems there can be no solution. The path of personal liberation not only provides us with a clear view of the sources of suffering, it also gives us the solution. However, we must continue on through the other three noble truths in order to learn how to apply that solution to suffering, so that we may be liberated from the bondage of samsara forever.

2. THE TRUTH OF THE CAUSE OF SUFFERING

Once the fact that suffering exists has been recognized, we then need to find the root cause of suffering. The sages say that the origin of suffering must be removed by its root, totally and completely, in order to liberate oneself from the ocean of suffering. If we are unaware of the precise root cause of our suffering, we attempt to alleviate our suffering by simply working to remove the most obvious and gross sources of our unhappiness.

There are many analogies that we can use to demonstrate how futile such a process can be. In one sense, it is like a doctor who only treats the symptoms of a disease but never attempts to find a cure so the symptoms keep returning. The ordinary person experiences the diseases of desire, attachment, and ignorance as the symptoms of anxiety, stress, anger, sickness, and loneliness. Trying to avoid the suffering of the symptoms without dealing with the root cause will only yield temporary results at best. The root sickness still remains.

Another way to think of this second truth, the need to find the root cause of our suffering, is that it is like weeding a lawn: trying to remove weeds from your lawn by simply cutting the grass is terribly ineffective. In a way it does work, because from a distance the lawn looks uniformly green. But upon only slightly closer inspection, it becomes obvious that the lawn is not uniformly healthy. Only one day later, it is even more obvious because the weeds have grown up much taller than the grass. At this point, the energy spent on mowing is clearly wasted unless we apply some other approach. The weeds will quickly grow back because the roots are still there. Everyone knows that we must use special techniques, such as pulling them out by the roots or spraying them with weed killer, in order to truly remove them. We must treat our suffering in the same manner. We must dig out or kill the very root from which our sufferings grow.

Yet another way for us to realize just how ridiculous are the mundane, symptom-relief approaches to suffering is to simply think of our relationship to our shoes and the ground upon which we walk. Imagine what life would be like if we spent our entire lifetime with no protection whatsoever for our feet—no shoes, no socks. We would suffer almost constantly from cold, soreness, and injuries. It would be impossible to protect our feet by completely covering the surface of the earth and everything on the earth with padding and leather so that our feet do not get hurt, uncomfortable, or cold. This would be like trying to put shoes on the world.

We know that putting shoes on the world is not just ridiculous but impossible, so instead we put shoes on our feet. However, when we attempt to surround ourselves with only the things that make us happy and never allow ourselves to come near those things that seem to cause our suffering, it is just like trying to put shoes on the world. Rather than attempting to distance ourselves from the superficial causes of suffering, we must instead protect ourselves from suffering by addressing its root causes, which are the three poisons of desire, attachment, and aversion. When we cleanse ourselves of the three poisons, we can experience anything that the world has to offer and still not experience suffering. In this way, we can say that addressing the cause of suffering is like putting shoes on our feet so that no matter where we walk our feet are always happy!

It is important to say a few things about karma at this point. Many practitioners think that they must simply purify themselves of all past negative karma so that they no longer have to experience the negative effects of that karma. Where the ignorant notion of the inherent existence of the self remains, there suffering will also remain. As soon as we believe in a real and existent self, we immediately also create a false duality of "I" which then naturally must compete with everything else in the world that we see as "other."

This false duality is the very source of our desire, attachment, and aversion. We then think, speak, and act in ways that are rooted in those three poisons. These unvirtuous thoughts, words, and actions in turn create even more negative karma. So, as fast as we purify ourselves of karma, we replace it just as quickly, locking us into the cycle of life that defines samsara. Therefore, again, although we can try to avoid suffering by avoiding the superficial causes completely, this just tends to reinforce the delusion of self which, over time, only creates more suffering than if we had not acted to avoid suffering to begin with.

Just as with the first noble truth, this can seem very dark and depressing upon first analysis. But as we explained about the first noble truth, we cannot truly find a way to peace and nirvana until we fully realize the causes of suffering. Only when we know the precise cause of our suffering can we then apply whatever measures are necessary for both short-term relief from that suffering and long-term solutions that enable us to permanently remove the cause itself and be free of all suffering forever.

3. THE TRUTH OF THE CESSATION OF SUFFERING

When we initially hear the first two noble truths, we may think that this fundamental and foundational worldview as advocated by the Buddhists is terribly dark. However, there is no way we can find a solution that ends our suffering without first knowing that we are suffering in the sense explained by the first noble truth. Even then, we still cannot find that solution unless we also know what the root cause of that suffering is; otherwise, we are just treating symptoms instead of applying a cure, as explained by the second noble truth. Therefore, once we are truly convinced of these first two noble truths, we are then ready to hear a third, that there is a solution that ends all suffering completely and forever. We call this fact the third noble truth, the cessation of suffering.

The previous section on the second truth described how to find the root of our suffering and explained that the root of suffering is always the ignorance that creates the false duality of "I" and "other." This ignorant view then pollutes our minds with the three poisons of desire, attachment, and aversion. When we take a good hard look at our suffering, the important thing for us to focus upon at this point is not how dark and painful life in samsara truly is. Rather, our focus now needs to shift to the fact that, if we have discovered the root causes and conditions to any phenomenon of suffering that arises, we are also on the brink of a solution. All we need to do is remove the causes and conditions that allow any phenomenon to appear, and it will no longer have a support for its apparent existence. If we remove the root cause of the experience of suffering, then cessation becomes not just possible; rather, the suffering must disappear because there is no longer a cause for it.

It is important for the student to understand that this solution, although surely effective, is gradual. When we first realize that we must completely cleanse ourselves of all ignorance, as well as the desire, attachment, and aversion that ignorance inspires, we may feel that although we now have a solution, it is a solution that seems almost impossible to execute because of the breadth and depth of its scope. It is best to simply focus on beginning some practice, no matter how small or elementary.

If that practice is then maintained consistently for even a short amount of time such as a month or more, students should begin to see at least small improvements not only in their ability to practice but also in the quality of their daily lives, meaning how much they suffer and how skillfully they handle that suffering. These improvements allow students to see more benefit in practice and to gain even more benefit from continued practice. However, in the earliest stages, it is also incredibly important for any improvements a student notices to be recognized as reasons to have greater faith and confidence in the dharma in general and in this third noble truth, the cessation of suffering, in particular. It is easier to see that it is indeed possible to remove the roots of suffering and find cessation when we begin dharma practice and almost immediately begin to suffer less.

It is also easier to believe confidently in the cessation of suffering if we look to the examples of the many beings throughout history who have reached the ultimate goal of liberation from their own suffering. When we have doubts about our own practice and its ability to lead us to the cessation of suffering, we should spend some time in contemplation of all those sages that came before us. They were once ignorant, just like us.

They experienced desire, attachment, and aversion, just like us. They began a practice, just like us. However, unlike us, they cleansed themselves of their ignorance and thus found cessation of their suffering. Therefore, if we stay with our practice long enough, just like they did, we too may find cessation of our suffering. When we look up to the historical figures that attained the goal for which we have only begun to strive, it helps to energize ourselves and our practice so that we have the diligence and perseverance to continue on the path in the face of obstacles.

4. The Truth of the Path

The fourth noble truth is the truth of the path. We have identified the first three truths and have a firm grasp of the fact that suffering exists, that suffering has a cause, and that it is possible for suffering to cease if we eliminate that cause. The fourth noble truth explains that there is a specific solution, a particular method that we can use to eliminate the root cause of our suffering so that we may become completely free from the bondage of samsara. That method is known as the noble eightfold path.

THE NOBLE EIGHTFOLD PATH.

CALLIGRAPHY BY LAMA DUDJOM DORJEE.

3. The Noble Eightfold Path

I N THE FIRST turning of the wheel of dharma, Shakyamuni Buddha laid out the solution to the problem of suffering very clearly in a program of practice known as the noble eightfold path. The eightfold path teaches us that we should spend our lives engaging our body, speech, and mind in rigorous and diligent practice of the following:

1. Right view
2. Right thought
3. Right speech
4. Right action
5. Right livelihood
6. Right effort
7. Right mindfulness
8. Right concentration

These may seem very general or esoteric, but with just a small amount of commentary on each of the eight components of the path, we get a very clear idea of what we should do to accomplish the ultimate goal of liberation.

1. Right View

Right view, also called right understanding, is the ability to understand the nature of things exactly as they are, without delusion or distortion. If we hold wrong views, thus misunderstanding the nature of reality, then our thoughts, speech, and actions issue forth from this misunderstanding. This in turn brings unhappiness and suffering. If we cultivate the right view of reality then our thoughts, speech, and actions are born from this right understanding. This brings happiness and freedom from suffering.

Imposing our self-centered desires, needs, expectations, or fears onto our perception or experience of life comes from wrong understanding. This is most easily seen when we are satisfied or happy when things go our way but are angry, sad, or otherwise unsettled when they do not. When our view of reality comes to us filtered through our own selfishness, our perception of reality is colored in ways that leave us deluded and confused. This results in actions of body, speech, and mind that cause pain and suffering because they flow from our own self-cherishing. However, when we have a correct perception of reality, one that recognizes the interdependent nature of all beings' happiness, our actions flow instead from a view that is altruistic at its core. This results in actions that are fundamentally rooted in loving-kindness and compassion, allowing us to find true and lasting freedom from pain and suffering.

With right understanding we correctly perceive the truth of interdependent origination, that all phenomena are both empty of inherent existence and impermanent. We realize that lasting happiness and satisfaction do not come from any temporary external phenomena but rather from learning to recognize the very nature of our own mind and thus discovering our own innate potential, our own inherent basic goodness.

Additionally, when we have right view, we have faith and confidence in the karmic law of cause and effect. We understand that wholesome, life-affirming actions bring benefit to all beings, and we possess the certainty that unwholesome, negative actions bring suffering and dissatisfaction. Right understanding requires our full comprehension of the four noble truths, which explain the nature of reality.

Right view is crucial to the practice of the noble eightfold path because it is the *foundation* for the practice. Although there are seven other parts to the eightfold path, they each depend upon the first, right view. Without right view, we cannot see what is correct and apply that knowledge as we travel the rest of the path. A practitioner must have the correct view in order to escape from conditioned existence, known as samsara. Without right view, the practitioner is like a blind man who has been abandoned in the middle of the desert and left to find his own way out. Just so, if we do not have right view, then we have no ability to recognize what is right thought, right speech, and so forth.

2. RIGHT THOUGHT

Right thought, also referred to as right intention, means that our thoughts, feelings, and desires are in complete harmony with the correct perception of reality that we develop through our practice of right view. When our thoughts are informed by a correct view of reality, they are in accordance with the way reality actually functions. When we practice right thought, our thoughts and intentions are free from selfish desire, hostility, and cruelty. Right thought means that our thinking, attitude, and motivations are aligned with love, kindness, compassion, wisdom, and harmlessness.

Also, we unconditionally extend this altruistic mindset, these noble qualities, to all living beings. Like right view, right thought is also directly related to other aspects of the eightfold path such as right speech and right action. The way we think directly influences our speech and actions. Therefore, our misunderstanding of reality causes wrong thinking, which gives rise to unvirtuous speech and actions which in turn cause harm. This results not only in pain and suffering, but also in the creation of more and more negative karma.

The phenomenal world, as we perceive it, is the fruition of our individual karma. Karma is cause and effect, it is the result of action, and action originates from thoughts. Therefore, right thought deserves much mindfulness and awareness, because our thoughts set off chains of events that eventually create every aspect of our experience of reality during this lifetime. As dharma practitioners, we strive to dedicate our body, speech, and mind to the dharma path; however, our body and speech are ruled by the mind, which makes right thought extremely important.

By analogy, mind could be considered the king, and body and speech his subjects; if the king is confused and gives orders to his subjects that are negative in nature, then the subjects' actions to carry out these orders would have negative results and therefore create negative karma. In contrast, if the king has right thought, then his directions to his subordinates will result in their acting in a way that is positive, bringing benefit to themselves and others. Thus, it is important that our mind has the clarity and awareness to govern the body and speech, directing them toward positive action and the creation of positive karma.

3. Right Speech

Right speech is the ability to speak truthfully and without causing harm. Right speech comes naturally from right thought, since our speech is a direct expression of our thoughts. In the context of Buddhist ethics and the practice of those ethics as taught by Shakyamuni Buddha in the eightfold path, right speech is extremely important. This is because the words we use to express our thoughts can either bring benefit or harm to ourselves and others, thereby creating positive or negative karma. Therefore, practitioners must choose their words with extreme care. The Buddha taught four specific methods by which we can regulate our speech for the benefit of ourselves and others.

First, we should always speak *words of honesty,* meaning simply that we always give voice to the truth. Right speech means that we do not lie or slander, for speaking in those ways creates resentment, conflict, division, and disharmony among others.

Second, we should always use *words of kindness,* meaning that we avoid saying things that bring negativity, harm, and dissention. Our speech should never be cruel or hurtful to others. Our words should not create hatred, misunderstanding, or suffering.

Third, we must cultivate the practice of always using *words of nurturing and mutual respect.* These are words and ways of speaking that bring peace, harmony, and comfort. We should always refrain from speaking in ways that are harsh, rude, impolite, abusive, or malicious.

Finally, we must always use *words that are worthy,* meaning to speak what is useful and valuable for each moment. We must reduce our involvement in things such as slander and gossip that do nothing but distract us and waste our time and energy. We refrain from idle, useless, or foolish talk. In this way, we cultivate the ability to speak the truth skillfully; we learn to use words that are friendly, gentle, benevolent, and meaningful while still being honest, forthright, and truthful.

Right speech means speaking kindly and wisely at the right time and place. When we are not able to speak in ways that are beneficial, useful, kind, or uplifting, we may consider the wisdom of abiding in noble silence. Through right speech we cultivate ethical conduct and personal integrity, the essential foundations of the path.

4. Right Action

Right action, or right conduct, means that our behavior is ethical, honorable, and responsible. Like right speech, right action also comes naturally from right thought, since our actions are a direct expression of our thoughts. Our conduct, being in accord with right thought, will always be consistent with compassion, generosity, and nonviolence. We abstain from unwholesome behavior such as destroying life (killing), taking what is not given (stealing), or engaging in sexual misconduct. The Buddha taught that to follow the path of right action is simple: do no harm. Unwholesome actions lead us toward states of mind that are increasingly negative, whereas wholesome actions lead to positive states of mind. To have wholesome behavior, we must adopt the ten wholesome actions and abandon the ten unvirtuous behaviors. To do this at the physical level, to practice the ten wholesome actions of the body, is easily summed up in the following three simple parts.

Respect life

Abstain from harming sentient beings, especially from taking life, including suicide. We should certainly refrain from doing harm intentionally; however, through cultivating our own wisdom and mindfulness, we can learn to refrain from doing harm as a result of negligence. We should cultivate an attitude of respect and value for all living beings, and demonstrate this attitude by nurturing and protecting life wherever and whenever we have the opportunity.

Do not steal

Earn all that you have and abstain from taking what is not given. This includes acquiring the possessions of others through fraud, deceitfulness, or dishonesty. Rather, we cultivate our compassion through actions of generosity, giving wherever and whenever we see others in need of our material assistance.

Control desire

Do not take part in sexual misconduct by being overcome by your desire. Conduct all sexual relationships using kindness, compassion, and respect rather than allowing your behavior to harm another being. If you are an extremely advanced practitioner, then you may take ordination and become a monk or nun, one who follows the rules and regulations of the Vinaya Sutra. If you are an ordinary practitioner, desire may be controlled by following the lay precepts. The precept for lay practitioners regarding sexual conduct states that sexual relationships should always be monogamous in nature, requiring honesty and faithfulness at all times for the duration of the relationship.

5. Right Livelihood

Right livelihood requires that we earn our living in an honorable and life-affirming way, free from deceit or dishonesty. When we earn our living in a righteous way, our wealth is gained legally and peacefully, in a manner that avoids bringing harm to others and ourselves. We should not earn our livelihood in any way that involves harm, cruelty, or injustice to either human beings or animals, nor do we support those who harm other beings. Specifically, dharma practitioners should avoid dealing in weapons, raising animals for slaughter, or selling intoxicants such as alcohol or drugs. As a true dharma practitioner, we cherish all living beings and support and assist all life in general. Our main practice is to embrace our interconnectedness with all sentient beings.

Therefore, right livelihood means that we should engage in work and projects that create positive results, or positive karma, in both the short term and the long term. These activities should benefit not only us but also the community at large, whether we're talking about our own neighborhood or the entire planet. To be in accord with right livelihood means to live in harmony and unity with all life on the planet. Furthermore, we must live not just to satisfy our own personal desires but also to compassionately serve the welfare of all beings. By living in accordance with the standards of right livelihood, we greatly enhance our progression on the path toward the ultimate goal of liberation. Even small improvements in right livelihood during one lifetime are considered great progress for many lives to come; they are like drops of water that accumulate over time to eventually form an ocean.

6. Right Effort

Right effort is the wholehearted, diligent, and energetic endeavor to train our mind and heart. We are to renounce or transform negative feelings, thoughts, and other unwholesome states of mind. We are to abandon those negativities that have arisen in our awareness. In addition, we are to develop and maintain positive, loving, virtuous, and wholesome states of mind and heart. Right effort means we avoid being carried away by distractions and desires. We are to develop steady perseverance, making a firm and unshakable resolve to practice the dharma. We endeavor to express love, compassion, wisdom, and virtue in our thoughts, speech, and actions.

Right effort could be seen as a prerequisite for making substantial gains in the areas outlined by the other principles of the eightfold path. Without enthusiastic effort, whether right or wrong, nothing can be accomplished. For the creation of positive karma this effort must be righteous, because misguided effort will cause harm and therefore the creation of more negative karma. Discipline and joyous diligence in the application of right effort is the key to persevering on the path. The decision to take up the path to liberation must be firm and always executed with right effort. However, we should not be distressed by the thought that a new practitioner must perfect right effort before making gains in any other areas of the path. At first, any effort is good effort, and then, as the practitioner uses that effort to progress in positive ways, her ability to improve the quantity and quality of effort will also improve.

If we truly want to awaken and attain liberation from suffering, we must practice with enthusiastic effort and joyous diligence. By this we mean that we do not practice the buddha dharma only because we feel an obligation to ourselves or others to do so; and we certainly do not practice because we fear that if we didn't, we would be punished in some way. Rather, we practice with joyful enthusiasm because we are excited by the positive outcomes of our dharma practice. In this way, rather than draining us of energy and leaving us feeling resentful or angry about the time and energy it requires, our practice instead uplifts and energizes us more and more as we put more effort into it. It is at this point that our ordinary efforts truly become right effort.

7. Right Mindfulness

Right mindfulness, or right attention, means being attentive, mindful, and aware at all times. We should be mindful of our bodily actions, sensations, and feelings; mindful of our speech; even mindful of the activity of the mind itself. Right mindfulness means giving our full attention to that which is positive, life affirming, and beneficial to other beings. We are also to be mindful to stay clear of that which is negative, harmful, or destructive.

To actually practice right mindfulness, we must cultivate those states of mind conducive to our spiritual progress. In accord with right mindfulness, our awareness is where it should be, completely attentive to what is happening within us and around us in the present moment. We see things as they are, without distortion. When attention is scattered or deluded, our thoughts, speech, or actions may become careless, which in turn causes harm to others or ourselves.

In these situations we can practice right mindfulness by embracing our own negative karma as being the painful consequences of our actions. We maintain mindful awareness of the fact that these painful effects are, in fact, creations of our own previous actions, that we are merely reaping what we ourselves have sown and therefore have no reason to feel victimized or persecuted. As we practice right mindfulness, we are steady, open, aware, present, insightful, and serene in attitude; we think, speak, and act with loving-kindness, compassion, and wisdom. Practicing right mindfulness enables us not only to cease the accumulation of negative karma but also to begin to purify the negative karma from our previous ways of negative living. Practicing right mindfulness helps us to accumulate positive karma, the merit from which will only help us to move further and more quickly along our dharma path.

Mindfulness requires that we always remain present in each moment, that we maintain awareness at all times. Meditation trains us to cultivate mindfulness so that we may achieve transcendent awareness and eventually completely overcome the pain and suffering of samsara. Mindfulness should be practiced not only during seated meditation but also in all other activities in our lives, whether we are walking, eating, working, or sleeping. In order to bring every aspect of our daily lives to our dharma path, we must cultivate perfect mindfulness and awareness. When every action of body, speech, and mind is directed toward the practice of dharma in every moment, whether awake or asleep, then we have achieved the perfection of right mindfulness.

It was taught by the Buddha that mindfulness allows us to control the four frames of reference to achieve great understanding. These four frames of reference are the physical body, our emotional feelings, our ordinary thoughts, and our mental attributes.

Body

Focusing attention on our physical being can help us direct the mind away from the distractions of the world. By focusing on our breath, our constituent body parts, our movements, our actions, or simply the fact of our physical existence, we can experience calmness and clarity.

Emotions

Paying attention to our feelings, such as sensations or emotions, and observing them arising and ceasing in our mind allows us to realize that they are dependently arisen phenomena and are therefore lacking inherent existence. This means that they are neither permanent nor solid nor real. When we misinterpret afflictive emotions as being anything other than illusory, we become overly identified with the sensations they produce. We tend to say things like "I am angry," or "I am sad," when, in truth, we are merely experiencing a moment of anger or sadness. The anger or sadness does not really define who we are at our core, which is actually basic goodness or buddha nature. Understanding the illusory nature of our emotions helps us to break our habits of clinging to those feelings so that we no longer define ourselves by these temporary, afflictive emotions.

Thoughts

Just as we can observe our feelings arising and ceasing, so can we observe our thoughts in much the same way. When we turn the mind inward, so that it looks upon itself, we begin to see that observed and observer are inseparable, and gradually we become able to realize the very nature of our own minds. The mind itself is nondual. There are not thoughts that are separate from the mind itself, nor are there thoughts that the mind "has" as though it possessed them as separate entities. The mind and the thoughts are inseparable, like the ocean and the waves on its surface. The waves are simply an expression of the current state of the ocean, whether calm or turbulent. The waves themselves do not change the nature of the ocean itself. Just so, thoughts are merely an expression of the current state of our mind. Thoughts are both temporary and illusory and thus belie the true nature of our own minds. When our practice brings us to a point where we are able to transcend the dual conception of our minds, we are then able to overcome the ignorance that fosters the wrong view that also separates "I" from "other," creating that false duality which is the root of all suffering.

Mental attributes

Although our thoughts and feelings are dependently arisen phenomena, from the ultimate perspective, the mind within which they arise is itself also lacking inherent existence. However, it does have three specific attributes that can be identified. These will be explained in greater depth in later chapters but will be touched upon briefly here. First, because the mind lacks inherent existence, its nature is emptiness, meaning that it has limitless possibility for transformation in the arising and ceasing of phenomena. Second, because it arises from emptiness, its nature is also unobstructed spaciousness, meaning that it knows no barriers or boundaries. The third nature of mind is that of luminous clarity. Since mind appears, and phenomena such as thoughts and feelings arise within it and can be observed, we experience a variety of activity just as we observe rainbows that arise and dissipate in the sky. The luminous clarity can be thought of as being a light that allows us to see what is in the room. Without the luminous quality of the mind we would not be able to observe phenomena as they arise, nor could we perceive the space within which they arise; however, since we can observe them, we are able to learn to differentiate right from wrong and overcome the negative karma we have accumulated since beginningless time. If we come to know these attributes of our own mind through meditation, we begin to know the minds and hearts of all other sentient beings as well. This is the mindfulness that leads to transcendent awareness.

8. RIGHT CONCENTRATION

Right concentration, also called right meditation, is the means for training and centering the mind. Through right concentration we bring our mind, ordinarily restless and agitated, into a state of calm and tranquility. When regular meditation practice results in the cultivation of one-pointed concentration, a mental state of unwavering attentiveness, this is what we mean by right concentration. By training the mind in right concentration, we extinguish the fire of the delusional, self-centered afflictive emotions. It is essential that, ultimately, we learn to completely let go of these afflictive emotions, because their destructive thinking rules our untrained mind and results in actions that create pain, suffering, and more negative karma.

Through this practice of right meditation, we develop serenity and mental discipline as well as emotional stability. We also gain insight into the true nature of reality by practicing meditation.

We need to constantly remind ourselves that we are practicing right concentration. We are ceaselessly bombarded by the winds of desire that push us toward samsaric activity, bringing us more dissatisfaction and suffering.

Our skillful focus will help us to stand firm and direct our mind toward right concentration, which brings us peacefulness and tranquility. Single-minded concentration helps us to recognize not only when we have fallen off our path, but also why we have fallen.

Through this practice, eventually we even come to recognize when we are about to fall. At these times, we are then able to self-correct by continuing to practice right concentration and following the dharma path without hesitation or doubt. Therefore, we move beyond having to fall and learn from our missteps and instead avoid making mistakes altogether. It is through this practice of constantly developing our meditative skill through right concentration that directs us toward the path of liberation and moves us more and more rapidly toward enlightenment and nirvana. Right concentration leads us through the various stages of meditation into a perfect state of equanimity that is completely free of attachment, aversion, or indifference; it is in this state that we come to experience a new degree of satisfaction, joyfulness, and tranquility that stems from realization of the perfect purity of our own mind, and gradually we gain attainment of the highest wisdom that is the unity with our own basic goodness.

Right concentration is a fully engaged means of training the mind and heart to be completely present and open in each moment, without cutting ourselves off from others or escaping the responsibilities of life. Through right concentration we also cultivate mental discipline: without discipline we cannot truly realize right concentration, and without right concentration we cannot attain the ultimate improvement of wisdom. When we do attain this ultimate perfection of our own wisdom, we have mastered the practice of an essential aspect of the noble eightfold path.

Sarva mangalam!

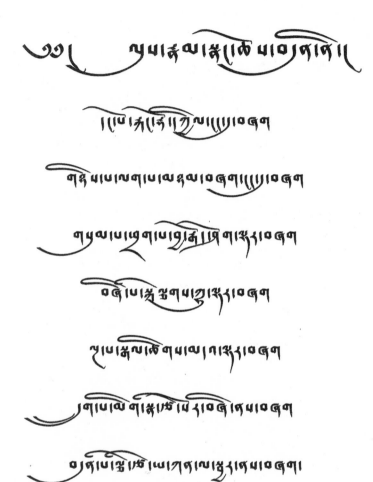

THE SEVEN VAIROCHANA DHARMA GESTURES.
CALLIGRAPHY BY LAMA DUDJOM DORJEE.

4. The Seven Vairochana Dharma Gestures

S HAMATHA MEDITATION belongs to the sutra tradition of Buddhism, making it an important part of the first turning of the wheel of dharma. The ultimate culmination of shamatha practice is attainment of the *arhat* state, also called self-liberation.

According to these direct teachings of the Buddha, we can overcome the very root of our afflictive emotions and achieve the perfection of ultimate liberation through the practice of meditation. However, according to the Mahayana tradition, we can only achieve this ultimate benefit of meditation when our motivation for practice is not only self-liberation but also the liberation of all sentient beings from samsara.

Meditation must be the core of our practice. From the very first moment we realize the necessity of embarking upon the spiritual path toward freedom from samsara, until the end of that spiritual path when liberation has been attained, meditation must never be set aside. No other practice will produce the end result of enlightenment, and all other practices or endeavors, whether spiritual or mundane, will benefit from a regular practice of meditation. All meditators, from beginning our practice of meditation until the time we reach enlightenment, should practice shamatha meditation.

Through the practice of shamatha we will gradually experience attainments in vipashyana, also known as insight meditation, until eventually we even come to experience the perfection of the arhat state. The development of insight meditation depends upon shamatha meditation. Without the foundation of shamatha, there will not be any real progress or result in vipashyana. Shamatha functions as the seed of meditation and insight is the fruit of that meditation.

In our early stages of meditation, vipashyana is not so much a practice as it is a result or experience produced by attaining a deeper state of shamatha meditation. Later, when we attain a certain level of stability in these deeper stages of shamatha, we can sit down with the intention of actually inducing the state of vipashyana and maintaining it. It is at that point that vipashyana has changed from being merely a result of shamatha practice into a meditation practice in and of itself. Gradually, as consistency and stability are cultivated in advanced meditators, these two methods are practiced together and are gradually unified until they become inseparable from one another. This is the ultimate fulfillment of shamatha practice.

PHYSICAL POSTURE

In order to become advanced shamatha meditators, we must begin to harmonize the physical body with both the mind and the subtle body of energy. We must align the physical positioning of the body with the mental practice of shamatha by using the postures traditionally presented as the seven Vairochana dharma gestures. The reason we adopt a very specific sitting position is that this allows us to become harmonized with our mother, the earth. When body and mind are harmonized with the earth, we are able to sit comfortably, in an unsurpassed natural state of relaxation and tranquility.

To begin refining our seated posture for meditation, we position ourselves on a comfortable meditation cushion. In traditional Tibetan Buddhist cultures, some meditators use a square meditation cushion which is four to five fingers high, while others can sit directly on the floor with no more cushioning than a small carpet or rug. For most of us here in the West, it is rare for us to sit anywhere other than in a chair. We lead lives that do not allow us much more than an hour each day, at the very most, for seated meditation practices. As a result, sitting in the most traditional meditation posture using the seven Vairochana gestures can be extremely uncomfortable at first, and may remain so for quite some time. But if we look to Asia and India or even to monasteries here in the West, we find practitioners who meditate so frequently and for such long sessions that their bodies become accustomed to the posture quite rapidly. In fact, after just a few months, the traditional physical posture becomes second nature to such a degree that their physical bodies can be completely comfortable and relaxed, leaving practitioners free to work exclusively on their minds.

Depending on the proportions of a person's body or even how much experience that person has with attempting proper meditation posture, some need their seat to be a little lower or a little higher. In fact, some people, due to physical limitations or lack of experience sitting without a chair, need to meditate in a chair or whatever it takes to feel comfortable yet alert and stable. There are two fundamental rules that we must remember regardless of whether we choose the floor, a cushion, or even a chair: our physical body should be (1) upright, and (2) comfortable. We must remain upright to cultivate a mental state of alertness. However, we should also make sure that we are at least comfortable enough so that our mind may focus on the practice of meditation rather than on physical discomforts or pains.

Once we have chosen an appropriate seat, we should sit close to the edge with our sit-bones firmly planted on our seat yet close enough to the front edge of the seat so that our knees can fall downward, away from our body, so that they rest lightly on the ground. This allows our body to form a very stable tripod base to rest upon. We should not have to lean to the left or right, or forward or backward. When we lean in one direction or another, we are required to engage different muscle groups to keep us upright. This will eventually tire those muscles and we will not be able to meditate as long as we would like.

That kind of leaning can also result in imbalances in the workings of our physical systems and our body's constitution, which will have the effect of creating obstacles to shamatha meditation. However, when we are perfectly upright, without leaning, our body feels light and the posture becomes effortless because our weight is stacked evenly. This also brings our body and mind into harmony with the earth upon which we sit.

Once we are seated comfortably, we begin to build our posture step-by-step, using the seven Vairochana dharma gestures:

1. Legs in vajra posture
2. Hands in the mudra of meditation
3. Shoulders spread like the wings of a vulture
4. Neck slightly bent like a hook
5. Spine straight as an arrow
6. Eyes gazing about four fingers from the tip of the nose
7. Lips naturally relaxed and tongue against the palate

1. Legs in vajra posture

Once you have settled your sit-bones appropriately on your chosen seat, place your legs, if possible, into the vajra position. We use the word *vajra*, which literally means "diamond," but this word is applied to anything that

THE SEVEN VAIROCHANA DHARMA GESTURES.
COURTESY OF THE AUTHOR.

has the attribute of being indestructible like a diamond mountain. Thus, the vajra position is the "position of indestructibility," in the sense that it allows the body to become extremely stable and grounded. It is known more commonly in the West as the "full lotus" position. To place the legs into the vajra posture, come into a cross-legged position in which the tops of both feet rest upon the tops of the opposite thighs.

This is not an easy position for most beginners, but with time and consistent practice the body will continue to open. Eventually, the body will reach a remarkable degree of harmony with the earth upon which it rests. There will no longer be any discomfort from sitting, only the deepest meditative absorption.

However, if the vajra positioning of the legs is completely unattainable, then the *sattva* position is also suitable. In the sattva position, the top of only one foot rests upon the opposite thigh, while the other foot is tucked under the other thigh. In the West, this is most commonly known as the "half lotus" posture. If even the sattva position is not possible, then place the legs in tailor position, in which the calves rest one in front of the other and the tops of the feet on the floor. Regardless of which of the three leg positions we use, it is essential for us to remember that both knees must fall away from the body and rest on the ground.

Because of differences in gender, there are subtle differences in the constitution of our physical systems. Therefore, men are instructed to sit with the right foot out and the left inside, and women with the left foot out and the right foot inside, creating a situation of balance for those physical systems.

2. Hands in the mudra of meditation

The second Vairochana gesture deals with the positioning of the hands and arms. Which of the acceptable mudras of meditation we choose will differ based upon our physical proportions (ratio of torso to arm length) as well as the strength of the muscles in our back and the height of our cushion. Each individual should experiment with the different recommended positions and adjust over time as the body opens and strengthens through consistent practice.

One option is to make a lightly held fist with each hand, but with the thumb tucked into the inside of fingers, and far enough into the fist that each ring finger is resting upon the thumbnail. Then we rest this light fist on the knees, palm down and knuckles up. Another position is to simply rest the hands, palms open and facing down, upon the knees. In both of these first two positions of the hands and arms we have created a tripod made up of the spine and the two arms. This is a very stable form for the body to take, and is thus the best to use for beginners and intermediate-level practitioners.

If we have been practicing long enough that we have developed a significant measure of strength and stability in the body, particularly in the back, there is a third mudra that may be used. With the hands open and palms turned upward, simply rest the hands one upon the other. The thumb-tips should only slightly touch, and the hands should be held just barely below the level of the navel.

3. Shoulders spread like the wings of a vulture

The third Vairochana gesture is known as "vulture wings." This position is used very little among most meditators because it requires a high degree of physical strength and experience. It is, however, used extensively in more advanced Vajrayana practices such as the traditional secluded three-year retreat or even the famous lifelong mountain retreats. Nonetheless it should be explained here because it can, with much consistent practice, eventually be brought into use with great benefit to our degree of awareness and alertness during meditation.

To bring the body into the position of "vulture wings" we make the same thumb-tucked fist that was described above in the second section on the mudra of meditation. We then bend the wrist so that we may take the back of the wrist bones and press them firmly into the hip-crease (where the thigh meets the torso). We continue to press the wrists down until they force the shoulders to rise and move upward toward the ears. This makes the meditator resemble a vulture, whose wingtips stick up above its head when perched. This causes the spine to become extremely straightened and erect, greatly heightening feelings of awareness and clarity and allowing energy to flow freely and naturally in the subtle body.

If the "vulture wings" position cannot be used comfortably, we simply maintain a position of equanimity in the shoulders. This is much more commonly practiced. The shoulders should be neither so far forward that the back rounds and the shoulders slouch, nor so far back that the chest bows out and forward. Also, the shoulders should not be drawn up toward the ears using the neck and shoulder muscles, for this only creates more tension in the body. If the hands are resting on the knees in the tripod position described above, it is most important that the meditator feel a sense of stability and alert comfort when engaged in seated meditation practice.

4. Neck slightly bent like a hook

For the fourth position, the chin should be tucked only slightly toward the throat, so that the chin and the front of the neck, or throat, form a hooked shape. This tucking of the chin is called *jalandhara bandha* in Sanskrit. The fundamental guiding principle behind the position of the neck and head (which will be covered in greater detail below) is that there should be a straight line that is formed from the root chakra, just below the tailbone, all the way up through the spine to the crown chakra. It is extremely important for the meditator to have just the right amount of forward tilt to the head, for if the mind is overcome by darkness, drowsiness, and dullness, adjusting the head's forward tilt by slightly raising the chin, and therefore the gaze, will help us to become more alert and focused on our chosen object of meditation. However, if the mind's attention is scattered and unfocused, simply lowering the chin slightly toward the chest will calm the mind and allow it to rest one-pointedly.

This presents us with a dilemma: we must first try to strike a balance, a place where the positioning of our own individual head is most conducive to a focused and productive meditation session. But, we must not get too caught up in obsessing over the positioning of our heads, for ultimately, a great meditator would be able to practice regardless of the angle of his gaze or the placement of his chin.

5. Spine straight as an arrow

It is important that the head, the vertebrae of the neck and back, and the tailbone all be properly aligned so that they become straight as an arrow. The arrow's head rests at the top of the spine which itself forms the shaft that is perfectly straight all the way down to the "feathers" of the hips. We should not attempt to straighten the spine by stacking the bones of the head and neck like a child's tall stack of blocks that wobbles and eventually falls. This depends too much upon muscular tension struggling against the pull of gravity. Instead, we should draw the crown of the head upward as though it is connected to a string that is being pulled upward. This will allow the meditator's head and torso to feel light and comfortably erect rather than heavy and sinking, which in turn will allow the meditator's mind to experience restfulness and tranquility.

It is extremely important to note that keeping the spine straight is not only guided by the purpose of establishing a posture that is physically comfortable yet stable. At a fundamental level, the most important reason to sit with the spine established in a straight line that runs from root to crown chakra is to allow a proper movement, or flow, of *prana* ("life force") and *bindu* ("drops") through the *nadis* ("channels") of the subtle body. The existence of this subtle body, also known as the energetic body, is a key principle in many theories of meditation. When the subtle body is harmonized so that energy can flow properly and unimpeded, the mind also settles into a natural state that is the ultimate goal of meditation.

6. Eyes gazing about four fingers from the tip of the nose

The sixth Vairochana position concerns the angle of the meditator's gaze. Traditionally, the eyes are aimed such that the gaze passes through a point in space roughly four finger-widths out from the tip of the nose. This means that the eyes are resting at an angle that is roughly thirty to forty-five degrees downward from their normal, level position.

This downward angle leaves the eyes aiming at a point about four feet out from the meditator's seat. However, the focus of the gaze should be softened by relaxing the eye muscles so that the mind's focus can be sharpened and directed at its internal object. Rather than looking with the eyes, we look with the mind. The eyes are neither concentrating on any particular spot nor aimed so close that they become crossed. Commonly, the eyes rest on a point roughly a foot or more from the face and, as the eyes come to rest, this allows the mind to come to rest in its natural state so that the mind's full attention can be directed at the chosen internal object of our shamatha. At the most advanced level, the mind is focused on formless meditation; the mind looks only at the mind itself. At this level the eyes are still open, but the gaze is softened to such a degree that no attention whatsoever is given to sensory input from the eyes.

It is very important that we be clear that this practice of relaxing the gaze and giving no attention to visual input is only appropriate if the object of our shamatha meditation is an internal one, such as breath, sound, or visualization. If our object of focus is visual, such as a statue, thangka painting, or the flame of a candle or butter lamp, then of course our gaze should be directed at that chosen object with one-pointed focus.

7. Lips naturally relaxed and tongue against the palate

The seventh Vairochana position is to let our tongue rest flatly in the bed of the mouth with the tip of the tongue curved gently upward to rest against our upper palate, where the front teeth meet the roof of the mouth. In this particular case, the immediate benefit is that when we properly rest the tongue in this way, we do not have to go through the effort and disturbance of swallowing again and again. This position of the tongue also serves as a mild cough suppressant.

There is another reason why a practitioner capable of attaining a deep state of meditative absorption for a significant length of time should sit with the mouth in this specific closed position. It is entirely possible that unwanted guests, such as insects, could move in and make a home in the nice warm cave that is formed by the meditator's mouth. To prevent this, the mouth should be closed so that the lips are gently touching, but with the jaw relaxed so that it hangs loosely and comfortably. Then we can continuously increase our meditative absorption without being bothered by the tension of a clenched jaw or the problems of a mouth that hangs open.

These seven positions of the body, the seven Vairochana gestures, are very highly recommended for practitioners of the Vajrayana tradition. They are common to all other Buddhist traditions and even to non-Buddhist practitioners of meditation. Most beginning meditators are not accustomed to sitting using these positions, and we all have differences in the flexibility and strength of our individual bodies. Therefore, some are able to get into and maintain the positions more immediately than others. Whatever may be the initial differences, it is important that these positions be understood and adopted so that we commit ourselves to practicing them. With consistent practice, eventually anyone can meditate using the appropriate recommended physical position.

PRELIMINARY BREATHING EXERCISES

Once we have brought the body to rest in a comfortable and stable position using the seven Vairochana gestures, we may then utilize a short breathing exercise, known as *agnisara* in Sanskrit, to calm and focus the mind. We begin by drawing the breath in slowly and deeply, in a controlled manner. We then breathe out, again slowly and with control, completely emptying the lungs of air. Then, we draw the muscles of the pelvic floor up while using our abdominal muscles to draw the internal organs of the lower abdomen inward as well as upward into the chest cavity, as though we were trying to make room for the bellybutton to touch the spine.

We hold this pelvic and abdominal lock for a moment, and then gently release it. Once the muscles of the abdomen are completely relaxed, we then breathe in and start the process again. This process may generally be repeated up to three, seven, or twenty-one times, and in extreme cases, even more, if the mind is particularly unfocused and disturbed.

ༀཿ ཞི་གནས་བར་ལ་བརྒྱད་ཀྱི་ས་ཁ།

ཁ་ལ་གཏོད་པ།

གཏན་པ་ལ་ཆུན་ཏུ་གཏོད་པ།

གུ་ལ་པ་ལ་གཏན་ཏུ་གཏོད་པ།

ཉེ་པ་ལ་བཟ་བར་གཏོད་པ།

དུལ་པ་ལ་བ་ར་གཏོད་པ།

ཞི་པ་ལ་ཞི་བར་གཏོད་པ།

ཉེ་བར་ཞི་བར་གཏོད་པ།

རྩེ་གཅིག་ཏུ་གཏོད་པ།

མཉམ་པར་བཞག་གཏོད་པ།

THE NINE STAGES OF SHAMATHA MEDITATION.
CALLIGRAPHY BY LAMA DUDJOM DORJEE.

5. The Nine Stages of Shamatha Meditation

According to the sutra tradition, there are nine stages of resting the mind to be developed during shamatha meditation. These nine stages can be considered a progressive series of steps in the development of shamatha from the beginning of our practice until we reach its perfection, a state of perfect tranquility beyond any concept or reference point. Toward this state of complete calm abiding, shamatha practice advances through three distinct stages: form meditation, formless meditation, and natural state or equanimity meditation.

This experience of resting the mind is one in which the mind is not influenced by any positive or negative notions. When the mind finds this place of equanimity, it is then able to either focus on one particular object or simply rest in its natural state.

Gradually we become able to rest the mind, which in turn allows us to also begin to recognize the changing mind. Recognition of the changing mind is a state within which the mind becomes aware that it is influenced by various thoughts and external stimuli. When we recognize that the mind has lost its focus on the chosen object, we immediately refocus on the object, which brings the mind back to a state of rest.

The experience of the observing mind not only recognizes both the resting mind and the changing mind, but it also recognizes the mind itself, that which is the observer. This is called the cultivation of witness consciousness. The experience of the observing mind allows us to attain the realization and conviction that the watcher and the watched are actually one, inseparable. This final realization is the ultimate accomplishment of the perfection of shamatha meditation.

Finally, we must consistently meditate using these three aspects of shamatha: resting the mind, recognizing the changing mind, and cultivating

THE NINE STAGES OF SHAMATHA MEDITATION.

DRAWING BY ROBERT BEER. USED WITH PERMISSION.

witness consciousness. Then we will gradually achieve the perfection of shamatha meditation.

STAGE ONE: PLACING THE MIND

We can think of our mind as a wild elephant being led along by a mischievous monkey. In this first stage, we simply do our best to try to catch up to that elephant in the hopes of someday taming it. The wildness of the elephant is represented by the darkness of its hide, which at this stage is completely black.

The first stage of resting the mind is called *sem jok-pa,* "placing the mind." This first stage of shamatha involves simply placing or resting our mind on a particular object or form. This might be an external object or an internal visualization. Regardless of what object is used, the first step is to simply place our mind's attention on that object.

This first stage could be compared to someone who is in the midst of a violent seizure trying to take a cup from a shelf to place it on a table. As beginning meditators, our minds jump and jerk much like the body of the seizure victim. However, if such a person repeatedly tries to tame her movements just long enough to bring that cup from the shelf to the table, eventually she can assert more and more control over her physical being. Similarly, if we try, just for a moment, to focus our mind, to concentrate our awareness on one object, that jumping and jerking mind becomes more tame.

This idea of form meditation can be approached two different ways. One may choose an object that is mundane, such as a candle, a rock, a color, etc. However, it is more traditional to use a sacred object such as a statue or thangka painting of a meditational deity as a support for our shamatha meditation.

STAGE TWO: PLACING THE MIND AGAIN AND AGAIN

At this second stage of shamatha meditation, we should notice a very small amount of improvement in the state of our mind; thus, we can think of the wild elephant as having a small white patch on its head. It is still wild, but less so.

This second stage of resting the mind is called *sem gyun-du jok-pa,* "placing the mind again and again." Initially, we are only able to place the mind on an object for a brief moment before our mind's attention wanders. This is the first stage of shamatha meditation. In the second stage, we realize that our attention has wandered, recognize this without judgment, and then simply bring our mind back to the object, continuing to attempt to hold it there with mindfulness.

At this stage of the development of our meditation, our mind's attention will continue to wander, over and over again, and each time we simply bring our attention back so that we are *placing the mind again and again* on the object of our focus. This second stage trains our mind to rest in a way that is a small improvement over the effort used in the first stage, when we simply brought our attention to the object and it immediately wandered away.

STAGE THREE: CONTINUOUSLY PLACING THE MIND

In the third stage of shamatha meditation, we can think of the wild elephant's head as turning completely white. This symbolizes the fact that the untamed mind has made some significant improvement, that it is actually becoming tamer after all.

This third stage of resting the mind is called *sem len-te jok-pa,* which means "patching the mind," but we could say that this means that the meditator is now able to engage in *continuously placing the mind.* Once we have developed the mindfulness to recognize when our mind has wandered from the chosen object of our attention, we then learn to recognize distracting thoughts as soon as they arise. As soon as thoughts do arise, we identify them without attaching to and interacting with them. We then simply allow these newly arisen thoughts to dissipate naturally without allowing our mind's focus to wander from the original object of our attention. Great meditators recognize that the arising of thoughts in the mind stream is not a problem for the quality of our meditation. However, problems do occur when we cling to these extraneous thoughts, for this clinging (or chasing) breaks our focus and destroys our meditation. For this reason, we must not allow these other thoughts that arise to distract our attention from the object of our meditation. We are then *continuously placing the mind* on one object for any chosen duration of time, thereby further refining our mind's attention.

In these first three stages of shamatha, our mind is so agitated that even the smallest successes are incredible improvements. This can be explained using two analogies.

First, our mind's focus is like a candle flame, delicate and easily extinguished. A single candle flame unprotected from the wind can be blown out by the gentlest puff of air. Therefore, it is almost useless for lighting a darkened room. In the first three stages of shamatha meditation practice, our mind's attention can be compared to this candle flame. The smallest puff of distraction extinguishes our attention and the candle of focus must be continuously relit. Eventually, in the third stage, we have enough of the winds of distraction blocked so that we can focus the mind's flame of attention just long enough to see some improvement in our ability to be truly present from moment to moment.

In the second analogy, the mind is likened to a river. Before beginning our meditation practice, our mind is a raging river, with whitewater rapids and waves that completely cover its surface. When we begin practicing shamatha, we develop enough presence of mind to at least realize that our mind is like this raging river and see the waves on its surface. By the time we begin to experience the third stage of shamatha, the waves have settled enough that we can actually see into the water, if only a little way below the surface.

STAGE FOUR: THOROUGHLY SETTLING THE MIND

As you can see in the illustration of the nine stages, when moving into the fourth stage of shamatha meditation, the white patch on the elephant's hide has spread from its head down onto its chest and legs. This further emphasizes the idea that the more time we spend practicing shamatha, the more controllable the mind becomes. The elephant continues to become more controllable, tamer; likewise, our mind becomes tamer because we are learning to intentionally assert control over it.

This fourth stage of resting the mind is called *sem nye-war jok-pa,* which means "thoroughly settling the mind." Because we have begun to stabilize and direct the mind in the first three stages of our shamatha meditation practice, our mind is now further clarified and rests more evenly. In this fourth stage, when we meditate and have brief experiences of samadhi (concentrated meditative absorption), we experience our mind becoming more open and spacious.

Before we began to refine the mind through shamatha meditation, we didn't even notice the gross distractions in our meditation practice. However, as the mind's concentration improves, even those distractions that are the most subtle, and therefore previously undetectable, can sometimes be recognized at this fourth stage. These subtlest distractions constantly escape from our samadhi, so in order to tame the wild mind even further, we actually constrict our focus to these subtle movements of the mind. We observe them continuously in order to *thoroughly settle the mind.*

STAGE FIVE: PLACING AND TAMING THE MIND

Continuing our analogy of the wild elephant, in this fifth stage we see that the entire front half of it has gone white. At this point, we could say that the mind is finally approaching being halfway toward this goal of becoming perfectly tame. Unfortunately, at this stage, halfway is still the very best that we can do, and some days not even that!

This fifth stage of resting the mind is called *sem dul-war jok-pa,* which means "placing and taming the mind." We already realize the extraordinary benefits from meditation for ourselves and for others. This is like realization of the benefits of taming a wild horse. A wild horse, even when corralled, does no good for anyone, and although potentially extremely dangerous to others, continues to use resources, such as food. However, once this horse has been tamed, the resources allocated to it show a return in that the horse can be used in a variety of ways, whether to do work, be ridden for pleasure, or even win races.

Just so, realizing, remembering, and reflecting upon the qualities of the stabilized mind generates a spontaneous experience of joyfulness, lightness, enthusiasm, and relaxation. Thus, it becomes a natural part of our practice to encounter distractions and disperse them by remembering the value of retaining focus and then settling deeper into that focus. Reflection on these good qualities that manifest as a result of our meditation practice causes the mind to rest and stabilize even more deeply. We then remain in this state of samadhi as long as we are able to maintain it, allowing us to even further *place and tame the mind.*

STAGE SIX: PACIFYING THE MIND

Returning to our elephant, we now see that it is mostly white; the only parts that are still black, or wild, are its hindquarters, legs, and tail. At this stage of shamatha meditation we can consistently rest the mind on our object of focus for at least half of our meditation session. This is because, like our elephant, the mind is now more tame than wild.

This sixth stage of resting the mind is called *sem zhi-war je-pa,* which means "pacifying the mind." We tamed the mind somewhat in the fifth stage in response to the lightness, joyfulness, and enthusiasm we felt in meditation. Yet there is still a tendency for the mind to wander.

We should think about cleansing the mind of its distraction as we would clean our dirty laundry: simply rinsing a soiled article of clothing in a little water will wash away the most obvious dirt and smudges, but the smaller, deeper stains require more work and focused attention, whether it be more direct scrubbing, the use of special chemicals and cleansers, or even utilizing the assistance of a specialist such as a dry-cleaning shop. Just so, once we have cleansed our minds of the most obvious and gross distractions, we must address the finer and more subtle obstacles to properly focusing our attention. The principal problem at this stage is that we are attached to the entertainment provided by those distractions and wanderings of the mind. The specific method we use to break that attachment and cleanse ourselves of distractions is not only to observe them as they arise but also to recognize the fact that they are harmful to the blissful and beneficial meditative state that we established in the previous stage of the development of our shamatha practice. When we recognize the faults and disadvantages of such distractions, they are naturally and spontaneously pacified and dispersed through the power of mindfulness and awareness. This allows us to *pacify the mind*.

MOVING DEEPER INTO SHAMATHA

The first six of the nine stages work mainly with the gross wildness of the mind. The last three stages pacify the most subtle aspects of mental dullness and agitation. It is important to understand that there are two aspects to the refinement of our attention in shamatha practice: first, our ability to focus and concentrate our attention on any one object, whether form or formless, continuously improves. Second, as our focus increases, our distractions decrease both in number and size. Not only are there fewer distractions but those distractions that do remain are smaller, subtler, and finer. They are in essence much harder to detect, requiring more and more from our constantly improving attention, as well as finer and subtler methods. These most refined methods are addressed in the seventh, eighth, and ninth stages of shamatha meditation.

STAGE SEVEN: MORE DEEPLY PACIFYING THE SUBTLER MIND

The image for the seventh stage of shamatha meditation shows the elephant now almost completely white. The only black that remains is on its lower legs and feet, and on its tail. At this stage of shamatha meditation, our mind is so tame that it can be used even more powerfully to finish the task of taming itself. Our attention can be brought to bear so powerfully that our focus is unimaginable unless one has actually experienced these profound depths of samadhi.

This seventh stage of resting the mind is called *sem nam-par-zhi-war je-pa,* which means "more deeply pacifying the subtler mind." At this stage we move past working with that gross wildness of the mind described in the first six stages, and we begin to focus on subtler distractions. Whereas before, in the first six stages, we have had some glimpses of these extremely subtle distractions from time to time, it is at this point, in the seventh stage, that we become capable of consistently recognizing those subtlest of distractions and smallest faults of the mind that occur during meditation. Because of the highly advanced nature of our practice at this seventh stage, even these subtlest distractions and obstacles are spontaneously liberated simply as a result of our awareness of them, and our meditation remains stable, as we are able to *more deeply pacify the subtler mind.*

At this level of shamatha, merely being aware of the obstacle is enough to disperse it. This is because, as explained in the sixth stage, we have already reached a point in the development of our practice where we are no longer attached to the distractions as a source of entertainment. We are able to let go of them immediately due to recognizing their appearance as well as realizing that they are harmful to our meditative absorption.

STAGE EIGHT: FOCUSING THE MIND ONE-POINTEDLY

Our elephant is now completely white. This symbolizes that, although there are still a few particularly subtle obstacles to perfect samadhi, the mind's attention has been perfected to such a high degree that all of its focus, all of its power, can now be directed to completely finishing the task of clearing away the very last distractions during the eighth stage of shamatha meditation.

This eighth stage of resting the mind is called *sem tse-chik-tu je-pa,* which means "focusing the mind one-pointedly." At this point, meditation becomes nearly effortless due to our familiarization with the practice of shamatha during the first seven stages of resting the mind. Those first seven stages were achieved through the power of mindfulness and awareness, and, as explained above, the result is that we begin to consistently notice and eliminate the subtlest of distractions.

In the eighth stage we develop the unshakable absorption that is required in order to work with and pacify the very last of those subtlest of the subtle distractions. This results in the near perfection of a subtle clarity and stability that moves us toward the ninth stage. Dispersing these last few subtlest distractions, doing this finest work with our own mind, allows us to truly find a meditative absorption in which we finally *focus the mind one-pointedly* almost without fail throughout the entire session of our shamatha.

STAGE NINE: SETTLING THE MIND IN EQUIPOISE

In the final image of our illustration, there is an important change in our elephant: not only is it completely white, it is also being ridden. This signifies that the mind has now been brought under such a high degree of control that it can be used with perfect consistency. A truly tame animal will never turn on or run from its master; just so, a truly tame mind will never wander or experience negativity.

This ninth stage of resting the mind is called *sem nyam-par jok-pa,* which means "the mind settles in equipoise." This is the stage when we become free of all distractions, whether subtle or gross, when our mind is resting completely evenly and balanced in samadhi. At this stage, the mind simply rests in perfect and unshakable equipoise beyond any concepts of good or bad, unswayed by desire or aversion. Reaching this stage, our mind's attention and focus are completely unaffected by circumstances external to the mind. These circumstances could be outer distractions present in our environment, or even internal distractions such as hunger or thirst, loneliness or boredom. At this stage of resting the mind, such distractions have completely ceased to appear at all.

In this ninth stage of shamatha, our samadhi is so deep that a sense of timelessness is developed such that the meditator can maintain the meditative absorption of this perfectly refined attention indefinitely. At this stage of the shamatha meditator's development, the state of arhat has been reached, and the root of the negative afflictive emotions has been not just cut but dug out forever.

It is important to note here that at this ninth stage of shamatha, the point at which a meditator reaches this state of arhat, full enlightenment and buddhahood have not yet been reached. In fact, due to the bliss of resting in perfect equipoise, the arhat is still tied to the three realms of samsara by his attachment to the state of samadhi he has attained. Granted, the arhat has indeed reached a neutral point, creating no more negative karma and unfettered by negative thoughts or actions. However, he also accumulates no positive karma, no merit from positive actions of compassion and wisdom. The arhat may rest in this neutral state of deep absorption for a seemingly infinite time until awakened by the compassionate action of the outreach of a great buddha or bodhisattva. Once this connection with the sources of refuge is established, the arhat realizes that only part of the journey toward true liberation and enlightenment has been made.

SUBTLETIES IN THE DIFFERENCES BETWEEN THE NINE STAGES

When one first hears the nine stages of shamatha meditation being explained, it may seem incredibly difficult to discern a clear line of demarcation between each of the nine stages. However, with practice and contemplation we come quickly to the realization that searching for that line is futile. The search itself illustrates a lack of understanding of the concept of the nine stages as well as of the practice of shamatha and the experiences that result from dedicated practice. There will be times when our practice goes smoothly and easily. At other times, our practice may be a struggle and the very idea of samadhi seems completely foreign to us. Until we reach the very highest levels of advanced practice, our experience of tranquility in meditation leaps forward and slides backward in fits and starts. We are never really completely at just one of the nine stages. Our practice tends to overlap several of the stages at once, depending on where our monkey mind is during that particular session of that particular day.

THREE GROUPS OF THE NINE STAGES

We can think of the nine stages in terms of three groups of three. In the first group we have the first three stages of shamatha. At this point in our practice, we may have days when we feel the experience of the third stage, and other days when we can barely make it into the first. Regardless, compared to the state of samadhi experienced at the ninth stage, when we are struggling in these first three stages we really haven't even begun to tame the monkey mind.

In the second group of stages we have the fourth, fifth, and sixth. At this point, we do begin to really bring the mind under control and have some small experiences of stability in the samadhi of the higher stages. We also still have other times when our practice is very much a struggle, more like the first three stages. We have smooth times, and we have rough times.

In the third group of stages we have the seventh, eighth, and ninth. At this much more advanced level our practice of shamatha has reached a point where samadhi is always easily attained and we are simply refining our practice to a degree so subtle that we cannot even imagine the subtleties unless we are actually already operating at those highest stages.

6. Benefits and Advantages of Meditation

BUDDHIST SCRIPTURE from the sutra tradition illuminates the advantages of meditation. According to an early sutra, which is quoted below, there are twenty-eight advantages to be gained from secluded meditation. These are the reasons why the tathagatas have devoted themselves to practice. Each of the twenty-eight advantages can be used as a guide in the development of meditation practice. What we mean by this is that although the original text seems to simply be a list of obvious statements about the benefits of meditation, there are subtle implications within these statements. When these subtler implications are pointed out and explained in commentary, they can help guide a student practicing shamatha meditation toward achievement of the ultimate goals of dharma practice. We hope that the commentary below does exactly that.

> Secluded meditation guides him who meditates. Meditation lengthens life. Meditation gives one strength. Meditation shuts out faults. Meditation removes ill-fame and leads to good repute. Meditation drives out discontent and makes for contentment. Meditation removes fear and gives confidence. Meditation removes sloth and generates vigor. Meditation removes greed, hate, and delusion. Meditation slays pride. Meditation breaks up preoccupations and makes thought one-pointed. Meditation softens the mind. Meditation generates gladness. Meditation makes one venerable, gives rise to much profit, and makes one worthy of homage. Meditation brings exuberant joy and causes delight. Meditation shows the own-being of all conditioned things. Meditation abolishes rebirth in the world of becoming and bestows all the benefits of an ascetic life.

1. Seclusion and Meditation

Secluded meditation guides him who meditates.

In order to maximize the benefits of meditation, one must minimize external distractions by practicing in a secluded place. Once a practitioner advances and has achieved a higher level of meditation, there is no need to practice in a secluded place because the power of external distractions has dissipated. However, until one achieves that level of practice, seclusion is a good support for beginning meditators.

To illustrate, imagine the beginner's mind as a battlefield disturbed by afflictive emotions and assailed by inner and outer distractions. Practicing in secluded habitats provides great benefit to the meditator because external distractions are minimized. Without these distractions, the meditator can experience the physical serenity of the secluded environment, which assists in calming the mind while bringing about peace and harmony.

When ordinary people are out in the world with all of its distractions, it is difficult at best for them to make decisions that are good and sound, decisions that are guided by what is truly most beneficial for all concerned. Decisions made in the world of distractions are frequently based on the distractions themselves.

However, when we spend some time in meditation, away from these distractions, and experience moments of peace and harmony, we come closer to the basic goodness that is the actual core of our being. Slowly, the more time we spend in this calm abiding state, the more our connection with this basic goodness strengthens. Then, when we are beset by the myriad distractions of the mundane world, we can be guided by our core, this basic goodness. It is then that we become able to make decisions and act in ways that are aimed in the direction of always benefiting beings in the best possible way, in every circumstance.

2. Longevity and Meditation

Meditation lengthens life.

Meditation helps to replenish the vital energy that is required to sustain the life and vigor of our human form. Think of all that happens in the mundane world, anything that our senses can perceive, as things into which we may invest our energies. Unfortunately, many of these investments are poor choices. Energetic investments are just like financial investments. We can put too much energy into the mundane pleasures and negative emotions of the external world. We then wind up feeling scattered and dispersed. We can eventually become like a person who has all of her money tied up in risky stocks. When bad financial times come around, and they always will, these risky stocks crash and are worth nothing. If all of our money is tied up in these stocks, we are vulnerable because when they decline, we are left penniless. Just so, when we invest all of our energy into the impermanent phenomena of the mundane world and those phenomena decline or require more maintenance than we have the energy for, we are left vulnerable. It is then that we easily become sick or even die, because we cannot recover from physical adversity just as the bad investor cannot recover from fiscal adversity.

Fortunately, just like economic investments, some of these energetic investments are quite safe, like a savings account, or even return a profit, meaning that we get more back from the investment than we originally put in. For instance, when we spend time and energy meditating to cultivate the tranquility of the calm abiding state, we stop the outward flow of our energy. This is like learning to save money instead of always just spending and making unwisely chosen investments. But better yet, when we meditate, what energy we have put out or even overextended begins to return to us. The external pleasures and negative thoughts and emotions of the mundane become less important when we regularly practice meditation. We begin to see that the mundane doesn't have much real value, or essence, in an ultimate sense. When we begin to have these realizations, we tend to start releasing our grasp on the mundane. As our attachment falls away and our contentment increases, our vital energies return to us. Then, when obstacles and adversity appear, we have the energy we need to handle them smoothly and wisely, without being dragged down into ill health or even death. It is in this way that the simple practice of tranquility meditation helps us to maintain and even lengthen our life.

3. INNER STRENGTH AND MEDITATION

Meditation gives one strength.

When we appear to have difficulties achieving goals or accomplishing tasks, it is quite simply that we are lacking in inner strength. There are always obstacles in our path toward accomplishment. If there was no karma that needed to be overcome for us to achieve our goals, then results would immediately come to fruition as soon as the thought of the desired end entered our mind stream. The result would spontaneously arise as soon as it came to mind. Although this does seem to happen from time to time, especially for great realized beings, it is only because the work that needed to be done to overcome the obstacle that was blocking the result had already been done; the karma had already been removed in some way. Also, in this sort of situation there is already complete confidence in the outcome. But for most of us, and most of the time, once we realize the need for a particular change, we must not only see the need but also have the inner strength to follow through on a course of action that allows us to be convinced of our ability to overcome the obstacles that karma puts in the way of our goal.

It is meditation that can build this inner strength when we lack what we need to achieve our goals. When we first repeatedly sit in meditation, we worry that we are wasting time that could be better spent on other things. Our mind wanders to those other things, and our progress is slow. However, every time we make the effort to sit, and then continue to make the effort to focus the mind repeatedly on an object for our attention, such as the breath, slowly but surely our skill as meditators improves and we begin to see benefits in our life off the meditation cushion. We become convinced that there must be some truth to what the sages have said about the benefits of meditation. From this conviction our confidence grows continuously, which causes our practice to improve as well, until we are satisfied that all that meditation promises is truly possible. With this level of confidence, paired with our constantly improving ability to focus the mind on its chosen goals, we become able to overcome any obstacle that karma places in our path toward whatever we decide we should achieve. It is in this way that meditation cultivates true inner strength.

4. Negativities and Meditation

Meditation shuts out faults.

By "shutting out faults" we mean that, as the mind becomes absorbed in meditation, we naturally and spontaneously seal our mind against any faults or negative thoughts that could manifest negative speech or actions. When we are not experienced in meditation it is as if our mind resides inside a house with all the doors and windows open, with cracks in the walls and leaks in the roof. This type of house provides no protection from unwanted visitors such as intruders or vermin. When we begin to see that there are some negative thoughts that come into our mind from time to time, we may resolve to try harder to keep them out. This is like shutting the doors or the windows. But the cracks can still let in bugs, even the tiniest of bugs that can eat away at the house until what little protection we have crumbles around us. Also, there are still leaks that, over time, let in other subtle negativities, just like water that seeps in and rots away the roof that protects us.

However, when we not only become aware of negative thoughts but also engage in the positive activity of meditation, we don't stop at closing the doors and windows. By taking a proactive stance against negativity through meditation practice, we mend the roof of our mind and seal the leaks in our consciousness. Meditation allows us to completely shut out all the negativities that would normally invade and rot our mind. Eventually, with more practice, the one-pointed focus we cultivate on the cushion begins to take hold in our daily lives. This allows us to remain ever-vigilant against the negativities that once plagued us so that we may rest more frequently in a tranquil and calm abiding state.

5. Reputation and Meditation

Meditation removes ill-fame and leads to good repute.

There are several reasons why simply meditating will eventually change ill fame to an amazingly positive reputation. When we engage in meditation in secluded retreat our minds, and therefore our bodies, are completely engaged in our practice. Thus we cannot continue to commit whatever negative acts have earned us such a poor reputation. But more importantly, when we practice extensively in a secluded setting, wisdom must surely grow. As our mind becomes more focused and merit increases, so too does our ability to contemplate the very nature of our own mind. We begin to truly experience being able to exercise mind over matter. Siddhis (unusual accomplishments) arise, our relative compassion grows into true bodhichitta, and we begin to ascend through the bhumis to become a great bodhisattva. Just as the great sages also began their practice in this way as ordinary beings to eventually become the great gurus that we look up to today, so too shall we eventually clean up our own name. The practice of meditation in secluded retreat shall surely take us ordinary beings, with all of our faults, to the same heights as well.

6. CONTENTMENT AND MEDITATION

Meditation drives out discontent and makes for contentment.

Ordinary beings, due to the fact that desire itself knows no boundaries, experience feelings of discontent far more frequently than they do those of contentment. Because of this, ordinary beings stay locked in a cycle of desire, acquisition, disillusion, and back to desire. However, when we meditate in secluded retreat, we begin to see the nature of mind itself. When this happens, we gain real insight into the impermanent nature and perfect purity of all phenomena. This view of ultimate reality produces a mind that can always be perfectly content in every situation, rather than only being content in situations that produce relative happiness and therefore momentary and illusory contentment. That momentary contentment is actually false contentment, for it too is impermanent, and we are just as attached to its pleasurable feeling as we are to the situation that produced our momentary contentment. We must be like the great buddhas and bodhisattvas who, regardless of circumstance, remain forever in a state of bliss and equanimity. This state can only be attained by meditation in secluded retreat.

7. FEAR, CONFIDENCE, AND MEDITATION

Meditation removes fear and gives confidence.

For ordinary beings, fear and confidence are mutually exclusive. When one is present in a specific amount, the other will be lacking in that same amount. Thus, to remove fear, we must simply cultivate confidence. There are two ways that this happens as a result of consistent meditation practice. First, at a more mundane level, learning to focus the mind with greater clarity and accuracy allows us to bring all of our faculties of perception and action into a higher state of functioning. Additionally, we become able to put a greater amount and more focused energy behind those faculties in order to feel more effective and confident in ordinary situations.

Another deeper way that meditation eliminates fear by stimulating confidence is by strengthening the ultimate view of reality. When a longtime practitioner initially begins to have glimpses into the nature of mind and the emptiness of apparent or relative reality, these experiences of correct view are only momentary. Unfortunately, most of the time, the relative view still predominates. However, over time and with established meditation practice, these experiences of ultimate reality become more frequent and consistent. The correct view becomes easier to maintain for longer and longer periods of time. Eventually the confused gaps between these moments of clarity become shorter and shorter until our confusion disappears altogether. Then (and only then) can the meditator have true confidence in this ultimate view. The impermanent nature and perfect purity of all phenomena give rise to a state that is completely free of fear. This progression is most easily described by a Tibetan story that outlines a phenomenon that many of us have experienced in some way or another:

> As I was walking through the forest at night, I saw a deadly snake lying coiled right beside me on the path. As my fear grew, I could see more and more clearly its stripes and the way its head swayed from side to side as its tongue flicked out from between its fangs. Just before I ran for my life, I remembered something. Earlier that day I had dropped a length of coiled rope somewhere on this path as I traveled along it.
>
> Laughing at my fear and my own mistake, my terror melted away to be replaced by confidence in the fact that this was my rope, allowing me to step forward and retrieve it. But as I picked up the end of the rope and it coiled around my arm, I realized that it was in fact a snake that I held, helpless and unable to bite, in my hand.

Only knowing the nature of our mind allows us the ability to transcend limitations in a way that produces confidence capable of truly exercising mind over matter.

8. Laziness and Meditation

Meditation removes sloth and generates vigor.

Here is a story from the sutras about two students during the time of Shakyamuni Buddha.

At a time during the life of Gautama Buddha, there were two young students who were classmates and friends. Although they were close, and at that time considered equals, one was very diligent while the other was really quite lazy. Years later, when they were both adults, they met again at a dharma teaching. A great mahasiddha was teaching in the area where the lazy student lived, and as the lazy student was walking along, he came to a place where a large crowd had gathered to hear the master speak. The lazy student decided to stop and take a look, only to find that the great being turning the wheel of dharma was actually his diligent classmate from years before. Although they had initially started out their education as equals, things had certainly changed for the diligent student.

The lazy student had to stop and speak to his former friend. He approached the throne and said, "Through your diligence and enthusiastic efforts you have achieved liberation and enlightenment. Although we started out as equals, I am still suffering in samsara because of my laziness, my lack of efforts in meditation practice. Therefore, now I can only venerate you by offering you these three prostrations."

This story gives us an extreme example of just how much further one can advance when one is diligent and vigorous in dharma practice rather than lazy and slothful. It is the difference between being a prisoner in the chains of samsara and being freed from all suffering forever.

The stillness and tranquility that most associate with meditation would not seem to result in making one energetic. Viewed from the outside, it would be easy to see why one could get the impression that the opposite could be true. But in fact, there are so many reasons why meditation helps one to eliminate sloth and generate vigor.

First, we should examine why a lack of effort in meditation practice will actually make one even more slothful than ever. Upon learning of the importance of meditation as the only path to liberation, some then choose to continue along their mundane path anyway. These people, upon learning of both the problem of suffering and the solution, then make the decision to ignore both. They choose instead to just continue doing things the same way they always have, or maybe even to do nothing at all. This type of mindset and behavior reinforces a habitual pattern of sloth in an extremely acute way. Also, without meditation, one's thoughts cascade into the mind at a rate that keeps one from being able to focus on what is truly important. When this happens, very little gets done and much of what does get done is frivolous or pointless. Without meditation practice we spend much time caught up in useless activities of body, speech, and mind.

Upon hearing of the priceless value of meditation practice we should take this information and use it to fuel our practice. We should become excited by the possibility of self-liberation and use this excitement to empower our diligence in applying ourselves to rigorous and frequent practice. In short, we should use this to fuel our vigor. When we see the possibilities inherent in dharma practice and then use them as motivation to practice more, we set up a positive habitual pattern that eliminates sloth and improves our vigor. When this sort of behavior becomes a habit, it benefits every aspect of our lives, mundane and spiritual. As the cascade of thoughts slows down as a result of our practice, we are better able to see what is truly important and take truly appropriate action in response to the events in our lives.

9. The Three Poisons and Meditation

Meditation removes greed, hate, and delusion.

The afflictive emotions of greed, hate, and delusion are essentially synonymous with the three poisons of desire, aversion, and ignorance. Thus, they are easily treated by the antidote of a regular practice of shamatha meditation.

The first two poisons are really just a result of the third. When we hold in our minds the ignorant and false view that there exists a duality that separates ourselves from all other beings, we are caught in the flawed mindset of "I" and "other." Due to our own ignorant belief in the apparent, relative reality of samsara, we get caught up in our egotistical notion of self. The ego tells us that we must protect the existence of this self, and we start to pursue the objects of our desires, our wants and needs as individuals. This inevitably leads to varying degrees of greed, as we almost always place our own desires before those of others. Our own wants and needs always seem more important than the wants and needs of others.

Even if we do manage to cultivate some small amount of altruism, we tend to work to benefit others, to help them realize some of their desires, only after our own desires have first been met. This same ignorant notion of self is the source of hatred, or aversion, because anything that this flawed notion of self identifies as unpleasant we will work to avoid. Also, any other being that gets in the way of our accumulation of the objects of our desire will be identified as someone deserving of our hatred, to lesser or greater degree.

When we engage in a consistent practice of shamatha meditation we begin to break down our own ignorance. When we search for this self that is separate from all other beings, we are unable to find proof of the inherent existence of this "I" that is so much more important than "others." Through meditation practice we eventually gain some degree of realization of the emptiness of self.

Then, we begin to see the inseparability between ourselves and all other beings. When we develop confidence in this realization, it becomes impossible to continue thinking and acting in ways that are selfish or self-centered. We naturally and spontaneously experience an increase in our loving-kindness and compassion toward all sentient beings. This eliminates our own tendencies toward desire and greed.

This experience of the breakdown of duality and the realization of the false separation of "I" and "other" leads us to a realization of oneness with all beings that completely precludes any possibility of aversion or hatred. Using shamatha meditation practice as the antidote, we are eventually able to completely counteract the three poisons of desire, aversion, and ignorance. We can eliminate our greed, hatred, and delusion, thereby digging out the very root of cyclic existence.

10. Pride and Meditation

Meditation slays pride.

The majority of practitioners have a great deal of confidence in their own knowledge of the mundane world and how to make accomplishments in relative reality. Most are quite willing to offer up their opinions on any number of topics and to give their advice, solicited or not, on just about any problem. Once new practitioners have gone to a few teachings, or even just read a few dharma books, they quickly begin to spout off their own opinions. They may even try to explain what little conceptual knowledge they have gained to any other unfortunate listener who happens to get roped into conversation with them. Eventually, this same sort of person can even get to a point where he feels that his conceptual learning and small amount of practice amount to more importance than the words of a teacher or guru. He believes this even though the guru has actual realization of ultimate reality through years of actual practice. At this point pride has taken over to such a degree that the practitioner has gone beyond help because he very rarely recognizes how little he actually understands and just how much farther he still has to go.

Meditation helps us to neutralize this poisonous pride that keeps us from making progress on the path toward liberation. When we meditate long enough for our minds to settle a little bit, several things happen. First, we begin to see our own flawed behavior, tainted by the poisons of ignorance, desire, and aversion. We also get a more objective view of just how little good we do on a regular basis. We actually do a very small amount of good, compared to how many opportunities there are to do more. There are so many opportunities of which we fail to take advantage. However, as we get more practice cultivating a more tranquil mind through meditation, our mind becomes like a raging river that has begun to grow still: the mud in the water begins to settle to the bottom and we can more easily see into the water. Over time we may actually be able to see to the bottom, to the riverbed itself. Unfortunately, the riverbed is frequently littered with the trash and debris of negative thoughts and emotions, but once we have seen this, our pride will not be so much in our way. Only then may we begin the real work of cleaning up the mind's negativities. As long as our own pride stands in the way we cannot even see that the work needs to be done.

At an even more advanced level we sit and meditate on the nature of our own perceptions of apparent reality. We also may begin to meditate on the nature of mind itself. When we begin to practice at this level it quickly becomes obvious to us that we know very little indeed.

More importantly, it becomes even clearer that all of our mundane knowledge of apparent reality, even our conceptual knowledge of spiritual matters such as dharma, really is quite useless when compared to the dharma of realizations that are achieved through dedicated meditation practice. This realization also helps us to cultivate an understanding of just how much we should appreciate and venerate any genuine teachers or gurus from whom we may receive teachings. When we compare our own meditation to what a buddha or great bodhisattva has accomplished over years of consistent practice, we are more able to see how much further we have to go and how much help our teachers can be as we move forward along the path. It is when we begin to see truly advanced practitioners, our own practice, and our own advancement in this way that we begin to truly uproot our own pride. Digging out the very root of pride itself is therefore only possible when we stay dedicated to meditation practice.

11. Distraction and Meditation

Meditation breaks up preoccupations and makes thought one-pointed.

For most of us, once we have settled our minds on any given task and begun the process of trying to execute that task, we then go into a state of mind that is like a sort of autopilot. We continue trying to accomplish what we originally set out to do, but our mind is really no longer on the job. Rather, we get carried away by countless other thoughts that distract us and disperse our energy from the task at hand. We lose the quality of truly being present, if we even really had it to begin with. This usually results in our attempt at productivity being less than perfect: the task gets finished but in a way that leaves much to be desired. It is also possible that the task doesn't get finished at all. If this type of distraction is particularly acute, it is possible that we will never even get started. This type of obstacle to productive activity can get in the way of mundane tasks as well as block our attempts to attain a state of meditation.

It is continued practice at meditation that is the solution to this problem of preoccupation with the infinity of other thoughts and activities. The more times we make the attempt to sit down and focus the mind on any given object, such as the breath, the more likely it becomes that we will succeed in experiencing more frequent and longer-lasting moments of one-pointed focus. With time and practice, these moments of one-pointedness become consistent and extended to the point that the practitioner can hold his mind on one thing indefinitely. It is at that point that the mind becomes like a deep, calm ocean with no waves or obstructions to its clarity. Although the hundreds and thousands of raging rivers of infinite thoughts may run into that ocean of mind, the ocean is so large and so deep in its center that the rivers at its periphery cannot truly disturb the calmness and clarity of the ocean's depths. When we practice meditation consistently we can become like the ocean because meditation breaks up the thoughts that preoccupy our minds so that we may become one-pointed.

12. The Ice Mind and Meditation

Meditation softens the mind.

When the mind repeatedly experiences the relaxation and spaciousness produced by meditation practice, over time the mind gradually softens. At first, we may not like the idea of our mind being soft, but let's think about the concepts of soft and hard in terms of water.

One way for water to be hard is when it is frozen so that it is solid, so that it is ice. A block of ice, if it were to fall onto someone or something, could cause much damage; it would at least hurt. Also, if we hit a block of ice hard enough with a steel instrument, it could chip, crack, or even shatter. Similarly, a hard mind, when it connects with things, connects with them in a hard way. Like the ice, it is cold, unyielding, and heavy. Like ice, the hard mind causes damage and hurt. The hard mind causes suffering not only for itself but for other beings as well, thus continuing to accrue more and more negative karma. But a soft mind connects with things in a way that is flexible and fluid, just like water that is liquid. The soft mind is compassionate and adaptable. Unlike ice, water can flow around things; water takes whatever shape it is poured into, so we can say that it is very adaptable. Just so, the soft mind has the inherent calm and peace to be flexible, to adapt to any given situation so that it can respond in the most skillful possible way, using both wisdom and compassion. When the mind is hard, the heart is cold; when the mind is soft, the heart knows warmth.

13. Nirvana and Meditation

Meditation generates gladness.

Without a sense of calm and spaciousness it is simply impossible for beings to truly experience gladness. Generally, we are surrounded by a whirlwind of mundane activity that distracts us from any momentary happiness we do manage to achieve. Also, if we do manage to find some source of happiness that makes us glad for a moment, we are almost instantly beset by some degree of fear of losing it. Then we are taken away from our enjoyment by our own efforts to protect or maintain our sources of happiness. Our moment of happiness is ruined by our realization of its inherent impermanence and our struggle to try to make it permanent.

Meditation can free us from this cycle of grasping, fear, and disillusion in two ways. First, at a more relative or mundane level, when we do manage to find some momentary reason for gladness here in samsara, it is the presence of calm abiding cultivated by meditation that allows us to abide in the moment without fear of loss or struggle to protect and maintain our moment of happiness. We can simply rest in the moment and enjoy what good fortune has come to us. Second, at a more ultimate or spiritual level, it is meditation that eventually frees us from any dependence upon samsara for happiness at all. It is meditation that eventually purifies us of all negative emotion and negative karma. Thus, eventually we do not need meditation to help us find gladness in our moment of samsaric happiness. Instead, through meditation we are liberated from samsara completely and have the ultimate causes of happiness that are free of dependence on circumstances, free of causes and conditions for gladness. Thus, meditation generates nirvana, the unshakable gladness at an ultimate level that can never be destroyed.

14. Venerability and Meditation

Meditation makes one venerable, gives rise to much profit, and makes one worthy of homage.

When we have followed the path of the meditator for some time, these three benefits begin to manifest in greater and greater degrees. First, we become somewhat venerable as a role model to our peers. They see our meditation practice and how it has benefited us, how we think and act in more wise and compassionate ways. When others see this, they begin to question their own mundane existence and maybe even begin to embark on a spiritual journey of their own.

If we continue on the path long enough we become a lama, or teacher, and are then able to work with and help these others on their journey toward liberation. At the highest level, we come to the end of the meditator's path: we reach enlightenment. It is at this point that we are able to spontaneously benefit countless sentient beings throughout limitless time and space; we become a buddha. At that point we are truly worthy of homage, worthy of the prostrations of others.

It is at this moment that we truly are able to give rise to much profit. As the great sage Milarepa, the king of yogis, sang in his aspiration prayer, we will have the "freedom, great resources, and happiness" that allow us to actually "always practice dharma and benefit beings." When we have come to a point free of all desire and attachment, we truly possess all that the world has to offer. While we are still caught in the chains of samsara we are unable to really have all that we need because, no matter how rich we become, we always want more. Thus, we remain poor at the ultimate level, no matter how rich we are at the relative level. This is due to our constant dissatisfaction.

The more we grasp and cling, the less of what we truly need actually comes to us. But when we have the contentment of a realized being, the riches of the entire universe are at our disposal to be the great resources that can benefit countless beings. It is in this way that meditation makes us venerable, giving rise to great profit, ultimately making us worthy of homage.

15. Joy and Meditation

Meditation brings exuberant joy and causes delight.

This implies that there is so much joy being generated in the mind of the practitioner that it is boundless, that the meditator is overflowing with joy. Also, the word *delight* is intended to imply that the practitioner is not just happy, but happy in all situations and activities, that he delights in all things and at all times because his activity constantly and spontaneously benefits limitless sentient beings without discrimination or exception.

Obviously, upon reflecting on the choice of these two specific words, we can see that these particular two benefits of meditation practice are for those highly realized beings, great bodhisattvas. We are talking about great sages who have reached a state of realization so vast that they truly have limitless and unconditional love for all beings, without exception. They have developed their altruistic mind to such a high degree that the benefit for all beings is boundless; it overflows and reaches out to all in need. The great bodhisattvas find their delight in all situations and activities because their love is like the sun. It is not as though ordinary beings do not experience some degree of love at different moments in their lives, particularly toward specific near and dear ones with whom they have relationships. But it is important to remember that this love is relative and limited, that it is conditional. We ordinary beings do have an intellectual or conceptual understanding of unconditional love. We even come close to experiencing some sort of unconditional love at times, such as a mother's love for her children.

But this love is like a candle in a dark room: it helps us to see, but only barely. A more advanced practitioner of meditation may begin to expand her limited, self-referential love to a less relative, more unconditional love. Even so, that love only shines out like a light bulb that helps us to see the immediate area in which we currently function. Unfortunately, a light bulb still has its limitations. Only the love of a great buddha or bodhisattva shines out with the radiant splendor of the sun that lights the entire world so that we can see clearly even on the cloudiest of days. This is why we can use the word *exuberant* to describe this level of joy.

By the same token, the delight the great sages find in all situations is due to this same sunlight of realization: their view of apparent and ultimate reality is as completely and perfectly lit as that of the sun. Ordinary beings have only a candle in the darkness, one that must be brought close to this thing or that in order to see it clearly, thus getting only flickering glimpses of specific spots in apparent reality that are momentarily lit by this candle. The more advanced practitioner of meditation may possess the equivalent of a light bulb with which to see her surroundings in relative or apparent reality. However, only the great sages have a view of ultimate reality that is clearly lit, as though by the sun, showing every facet and detail of appearance arising and every karmic cause and effect.

Thus, we can truly say that the fully realized meditator, one of the victorious ones, truly has the ultimate causes of delight, that he can find happiness and contentment in his view of every situation and every experience. This is the ultimate benefit from the perfection of meditation.

16. Emptiness and Meditation

Meditation shows the own-being of all conditioned things.

This part of the text tells us that one of the primary benefits of meditation is that it reveals to us the emptiness of inherent existence of all composite phenomena. What we mean by "conditioned things" is that all things are dependent upon causes and conditions for their existence, and that without those causes and conditions they will cease to exist. Thus, existence is conditional. What we mean by "shows the own-being" is that meditation eventually reveals to us that since there is nothing in samsara or nirvana that exists without the necessary causes and conditions, therefore there is nothing that comes into being completely on its own.

One of the shortest explanations of this view of reality comes to us in the songs of the great Lord of Yogis Milarepa, when he sings that all phenomena have "no base to rest on, do not coemerge." Milarepa is telling us that no matter how far back we look, we cannot find an original cause for something. We cannot find a base for a single phenomenon's existence to rest upon. Take, for example, our own existence in this lifetime which is due to the coming together of specific causes and conditions, mostly our parents. However, our parents' existence was a coming together of causes and conditions as well, as were their own parents'. And no matter how far back we go, even if we believe that we can start to trace our way back through the earliest stages of evolution, we still cannot find one specific thing that is an inherently existent cause. Something has always come before it to be its cause. We cannot find one specific thing, a "base" as Milarepa calls it, which started the whole chain of phenomena that eventually led to our own existence in this lifetime.

But Milarepa also says that things "do not coemerge." This means that, if we are not convinced that all things lack inherent existence due to their dependence upon other phenomena as causes and conditions, then the only other explanation is that phenomena must arise without causes or conditions; that they arise completely spontaneously. But this is obviously not true. There is absolutely nothing that we can point to that spontaneously arises with no cause whatsoever. In fact, if there were such a thing, then reality would be completely full of that thing because it would be spontaneously coming into existence all the time since it didn't need a cause. For example, if our existence in this lifetime has arisen completely on its own without any necessary causes, then more and more of ourselves would be appearing all the time!

Thus, as the root text here claims, we can see that eventually meditation will show us the own-being of all things: that nothing possesses own-being, that nothing comes into being on its own, and that all things are dependent upon other conditioned things for their temporary existence.

17. Enlightenment and Meditation

Meditation abolishes rebirth in the world of becoming and
bestows all the benefits of an ascetic life.

This last piece of the root text makes an incredibly simple yet amazingly powerful statement: the benefit of meditation is that it is the cause for enlightenment. It says here that meditation bestows all the benefits of an ascetic life. This means that through meditation practice one eventually attains the perfect mindset of the ascetic, free of all negativities, free of all grasping and attachment. When this happens, the meditator is no longer dependent upon external or internal phenomena for happiness, and therefore the chains of samsara are broken forever. One who has reached this state has become a buddha, one who is completely victorious over all birth, death, and all other phenomena in between. Kings and queens, politicians and generals, although they may conquer the entire world, are only victorious over the mundane. Only a buddha has conquered all phenomena and the afflictive emotions that they inspire. Thus, upon the meditator's practice finally bestowing all the benefits of an ascetic life, there is no more desire, grasping, and attachment to continue rebirth in the world of becoming. Meditation ends this cycle of birth and death and the meditator no longer moves through the various intermediate states, or bardos, that define cyclic existence. The chains of cyclic existence in samsara are forever shattered. Meditation, therefore, abolishes rebirth in the world of becoming.

THE VICTORIOUS ONES AND THE BENEFITS OF MEDITATION

As explained in the foregoing seventeen commentaries, these are the twenty-eight advantages of meditation which induce the tathagatas to practice. It is because the tathagatas wish to experience the calm and easeful delight of meditational attainments that they practice meditation with this end in view; so that they may dwell at ease; on account of the manifold nature of meditation's faultless virtues; because it is the road to all holy states without exception; and because it has been praised, exalted, and commended by all the buddhas. We call the tathagatas "the Victorious Ones" precisely because their meditation practice has been perfected to such degree that they are completely victorious over their own suffering, no longer ruled in any way by karmic cause and effect.

Of the twenty-eight benefits of meditation listed and explained here, every practitioner of meditation will experience varying amounts according to her own individual faculties and abilities. Realization of these benefits is entirely dependent upon the level of commitment the meditator dedicates to practice. Without practice, liberation is impossible. With dedication to practice, there are no boundaries to the limitless possibilities available to the practitioner, and enlightenment is assured.

7. Obstacles to Shamatha and
Their Antidotes

W E BECOME DISTRACTED, we daydream, we fall asleep, our minds grow dull. We have exciting fantasies, remember wrongs done to us, and our minds spin uncontrollably off our cushions. Every conceivable obstacle to achieving meditational stability has been compiled by the sages from earliest times, and for every obstacle to meditation, there is a counteraction, an antidote.

1. The Scattered Mind

The first obstacle to shamatha meditation is instability of mind. This means that the mind is extremely unstable due to the fact that it attaches to *any* thought that comes into the mind stream and then proceeds to get extremely excited and involved with the infinity of thoughts that follow. In this case, the mind's focus is extremely weak and fragile because there is such a high probability of thoughts influencing the state of the mind itself.

It's not just that thoughts *arise* in the mind, but that the mind is so accustomed to engaging with and reacting to those thoughts. This first obstacle is sometimes referred to as a wild or scattered mind. The mind is wild like an untamed animal; all it takes is one thought to disturb it, and away it runs. The mind is scattered like an excited monkey; it jumps from one thing to the next, and so it cannot be placed on just one object of focus and held there for the length of time required to achieve beneficial results.

The antidote to this first obstacle to shamatha meditation is repeated contemplation on impermanence. When we attempt to meditate and find that we are confronted with this first type of obstacle, the solution, or antidote, is to apply contemplation and meditation on impermanence in a very specific way.

Gross impermanence

First, we begin by contemplating and meditating upon the grossest or most obvious examples of impermanence. One obvious example is that of a new car. When we first get a new car, it is shiny and perfect. It runs smoothly and without any problems. But were we to fast-forward twenty years, we could find that same car is dented and pitted with rust. It certainly would no longer run as well as the day we first drove it, no matter how well it was maintained. It is possible that it may not run at all! But it's not as though this happened overnight. In fact, as the days passed, one after the other for twenty years, we probably hardly even noticed the small changes that slowly resulted in a valuable new car turning into a piece of junk. This is the simplest and grossest way of contemplating impermanence. Once we've spent enough time with these types of examples, we can then begin to refine our contemplation and meditation on impermanence by analyzing more subtle external phenomena, changes that happen over centuries, or millennia, or even eons.

Subtle impermanence

We can refine this antidote by slowly moving to even subtler, internal phenomena such as thoughts and emotions. We can recognize that the thoughts that arise and the emotions they spark are also impermanent. They come into being for a moment and then eventually they are only a memory that may even someday be completely forgotten. We have a saying that is quite common when people are in the midst of being afflicted by an unpleasant experience. We say, "Someday we'll laugh about it."

When, for example, our child does something like paint on the living-room rug, we are immediately motivated toward some emotion like anger or other type of distress. And it is usually someone else that says to us, "Someday you'll laugh about it." Sure enough, when the child is grown and we think back on that moment, somehow it has transformed into a pleasant memory that only gives us amusement, not anger. We can spend much time in contemplating many and various examples of the impermanence of internal phenomena, leading us eventually to complete confidence in our realization of the truth of impermanence of all phenomena.

When we contemplate the impermanence of anything, whether gross or subtle, external or internal, it occupies our mind in such a way that the mind gradually begins to slow down; it takes a step back from the thoughts that had previously seemed to dump into it at a rate that kept us from any experience of tranquility in our meditation. Over time, when thoughts do arise during the course of a meditation session we tend to react less emotionally to them, and the volatility and wildness of our mind is soothed. When we no longer react to our thoughts and instead simply observe them as they arise, then the mind has been tamed like a horse that, when wild, can only do harm, but when tamed can be used to ride. It is not the case that the disciplined mind has no disturbing thoughts, but those thoughts no longer afflict us like a disease that controls the very state of our mind itself.

Without thoughts, we would be dead, or like some inanimate object. When we meditate we are not trying to end all thoughts but rather to end our affliction by the emotions they inspire. When we obtain a wild horse, we don't kill it; we tame it so that it can be used for benefit. Just so, we must tame our minds if we are ever to be of benefit to all other beings.

2. The Dark, Dull, or Hazy Mind

The second obstacle to advancement in shamatha meditation is known as the dark and hazy mind, which produces sensations of dullness, heaviness, fatigue, and a lack of clarity and focus. The experience of this obstacle is much like being in a valley where, as soon as you begin to meditate, the sun begins to set and the fog rolls in. The mountains and trees around you, the entire landscape begins to become difficult to see clearly and eventually cannot be seen at all. As night sets in, the need for rest and sleep overcomes you.

When we try to meditate and darkness sets in, or the haziness of fog rolls into our practice, similar sensations overwhelm our mind. The heaviness comes on and we experience feelings that we need to rest or even sleep. The objects of our meditation become hazy and unclear, diminishing our ability to focus. Our internal vision loses its clarity and we are left dulled.

The solution to this particular obstacle is quite simple: the antidote for a dark, dull, or hazy mind is for the sun to rise. When the darkness and fog begin to set in, immediately remember the power of the three jewels and your connection to them. Take a moment to recognize that their power is stronger and brighter than any foggy night. Immediately you will have the feeling that the sun is beginning to rise again. You will know this because you will have the sensation that the oppressive nature of the dark and haze is lifting, that it presses down on you less heavily.

Also, your vision itself will begin to clarify and it will seem as though you are sitting in a ray of sunlight. It is as if the sun had risen again to scatter the shadows that darkened the valley of your mind and burn off the fog that has clouded your meditation. You have reestablished your connection with the sources of refuge and strengthened your faith in their power. This will help you to become firmly established in deeper and deeper states of samadhi.

3. THE SKEPTICAL MIND

The third obstacle to advancement in shamatha meditation is doubt, or skepticism. If we do not have faith in the power of our practice to produce positive results, then it becomes much more difficult, and sometimes even impossible, to realize those results. This is because having doubts about our practice is like trying to entertain two contradictory thoughts at the same time: our mind's power becomes divided against itself. On the one hand, because we are engaged in meditation, we are having the thought that practice is effective; however, on the other hand, because we are experiencing doubt and skepticism, we are also having the thought that practice is not effective, that we are wasting our time with shamatha. We can compare this to several situations. It is like not knowing which lane of a two-lane highway we should drive in, and thus simply driving down the middle. Although not knowing which lane to use and making an arbitrary choice has a fifty percent chance of accident, driving down the middle has a hundred percent chance of having a wreck! We can also see our situation of doubt in terms of arithmetic: we take a positive number of powers of faith and put that into our practice, but then take an equal but negative number of doubts and add that to it. What advancement do you get from this equation of practice? Zero.

The solution for the obstacle of doubt is to cultivate one-pointed focus, unshakable and indestructible. Thoughts made of doubt and skepticism may try to enter a mind that is already completely and totally occupied with a chosen object of focus, such as the breath or anything else. But there is no room for any other thoughts, positive or negative, in a mind that is already completely absorbed in one-pointed thought. Over time, other thoughts are unable to enter the mind at all because our ability to focus has improved to such a degree that one-pointed concentration is familiar; we have cultivated the positive habit of not letting anything else in.

When our focus becomes improved to such a high degree that we no longer let in the doubting thoughts, we should also begin to experience some significant and powerful results from our practice. These experiences from advancement, in turn, help us to see that there was no reason to be skeptical to begin with. This will increase our faith, helping to further fuel our practice itself. It also makes one-pointed focus even stronger, which continues to reduce doubtful, skeptical thoughts.

This process puts us into a positive cycle that continues to take us higher and higher into more advanced levels of shamatha meditation.

4. The Afflicted Mind

The fourth obstacle for shamatha meditation stems from afflictive emotions. These comprise an obstacle to shamatha because of the power of our desire, attachment, and aversion. It is these that produce the experience of afflictive emotions. Our mind is accustomed to the passions and aggressions that arise out of desire, attachment, and aversion, because of habitual patterns established over the course of infinite lives since beginningless time. In fact, we are so used to these afflictive emotions that we have actually become attached to the mental activity of the afflictions themselves.

The antidote for this fourth obstacle to advancement in shamatha meditation is simply recognition and contemplation. We can begin to rid ourselves of our attachment to afflictive emotions by recognizing them as they arise and contemplating just how damaging they are to the advancement of our dharma practice. Unfortunately, simply realizing the negative nature of our afflictions isn't enough to uproot them completely. We may clearly see our passions and aggressions and wish to end them; unfortunately, because they have been built from the habits of many lifetimes, we must work with great energy and diligence to completely end their power over our mind and establish ourselves in the stability of samadhi.

As long as our mind jumps around from thought to thought, driven by the power of afflictive emotions and the agitation that they produce, we can never experience the tranquility that significant gains in our practice of shamatha meditation create. When our shamatha meditation is disturbed by the stormy waves of afflictive emotions, the antidote is to engage in a structured practice of contentment.

First, we must see that our experience of afflictive emotions is based in some sort of craving. Craving can be produced by desire for something. It can also come from attachment, which is a craving to keep or even accumulate more of something. It is important to remember that craving can also be produced by aversion, which is the desire to avoid something that we label as negative. Once we have contemplated the root craving that has produced the specific affliction that disturbs our shamatha meditation, we then move to contemplation of the fact that, for humans, craving has no boundaries.

No matter how many of the objects of our desire we accumulate, it is never enough; we will always want more. Also, no matter what negative experience we eliminate from our life, once we are no longer absorbed by that specific experience of suffering, there will always be some new physical or emotional pain to arise and plague us. There is never any real satisfaction of desire, or relief from suffering, in samsara. So, once we come to a place of greater certainty about the source of our affliction, which is craving, and the certainty that seeking real happiness in samsara is futile, we attempt to practice a greater degree of contentment with what we already have.

This is indeed incredibly difficult; in fact, only bodhisattvas can practice true and complete contentment, because they have sufficient realization and clarity of view. However, even the beginning practitioner can begin to cultivate contentment by starting with the contemplations outlined above. Slowly, a more authentic feeling of contentment will begin to take root and grow. As contentment grows, afflictive emotions will fall away, leaving our mind freer to deepen our calm abiding in shamatha meditation.

5. The Referential Mind

The fifth obstacle to advancement in shamatha meditation is a mind that is referential, meaning that we tend to place value on others in reference to ourselves. If someone else makes us feel in a positive way then we value them and become attached to them; if someone inspires feelings of negativity, then we develop aversion instead. Our attachment to loved ones and aversion toward our enemies is based on referential values rather than on unconditional love and compassion for all beings that stands without regard to our own self-interest. For humans, almost all of our activities of body, speech, and mind are motivated in some way by the two factors of attachment and aversion. This specific type of attachment and aversion guides us when we are off the cushion and engaged in the mundane activities of everyday life. Also, when we are on the cushion and trying to meditate, most of the thoughts that arise in our minds spring from our attachment to our near and dear ones or from our aversion to our enemies. Thus, our attachment and aversion quickly become obstacles to any sort of one-pointed focus in shamatha meditation.

The antidote to this obstacle, this very specific type of attachment and aversion, is to practice equanimity and compassion. First, we must engage in a rigorous practice of equanimity by cultivating a less sentimental and more realistic view of our loved ones. We must see that our love for them is relative, that it is a product of our own reference point. What we mean by this is that we love them based on who they are *to us,* which is generally based on how they treat us, or how it makes us feel to be around them. If their behavior or even just their presence in our lives produces feelings that are pleasurable enough, we say that we love them.

By the same token, if we hate our enemies it is again because of who they are *to us.* Our hatred and aversion is a product of our own viewpoint based on how our enemies treat us. It is important to see that if our loved ones behaved poorly enough, or our enemies behaved well enough, they could easily trade places in our minds. In fact, there are probably people who call our loved ones enemies because of how they are perceived, and there are surely some who hold our enemies near and dear, for even our worst enemies once had their own mother to show them unconditional love.

Once we have come to this more realistic view of our loved ones and enemies, we must not fall into the nihilistic view of indifference toward all others. Rather, we must instead cultivate compassionate equanimity. All the great sages of Buddhist teaching agree that we must come to see that at some point in beginningless and endless time we have been or will be a mother to all sentient beings, and that at some point during the infinite stretches of time all sentient beings have been or will be our mother.

This helps us to see how it is possible to experience unconditional love for all. We must also learn to view all sentient beings with compassion, without regard to how they stand in relation to ourselves or others. We can do this by focusing on the fact that all beings, regardless of how we see them or how they treat us, wish to avoid suffering and maximize their happiness. We see this simple fact as something that we have in common with every living being; it becomes a uniting factor in our minds.

When we no longer experience the stormy waves of attachment and aversion toward our loved ones and enemies, we instead begin to experience a certain measure of tranquility produced by this equanimity. This combines with our strengthened unconditional and nonreferential loving-kindness and compassion. When we have equanimity combined with compassion, we have new fuel to take our practice further than ever before, and all obstacles fall away as we progress higher and higher into our practice of shamatha meditation.

DISCIPLINE AND MEDITATION

The root of the appearance of all phenomena, all experience, whether internal or external, is the ordinary mind. Therefore, we must discipline the mind through the practice of shamatha meditation if we are ever to bring our experience of phenomena under our own control. We can do a lifetime of dharma practice but, without the discipline of shamatha to tame the ordinary mind, it will all be fruitless practice. Countless recitations of mantra, attendance and participation in retreats, and receiving many great empowerments will yield no positive result if we cannot bring the mind to focus while engaged in those practices. That disciplined focus can only be developed to its full capacity through the practice of shamatha meditation.

BASIC GOODNESS AND MEDITATION

All beings possess buddha nature, a sort of luminous perfection of basic goodness that resides at the core of all living things. At this point in our development we may not perceive the full brilliance of that perfection, for clouds of ignorance, and the negative afflictive emotions that result from that ignorance, cover our basic goodness. It is important that we realize that our basic goodness is like the sun at noontime: no matter how dark and heavy the clouds that fill the sky may be, they cannot completely darken the light of the sun. Just so, no matter how heavy and dark the obscurations to our basic goodness, they can never completely block the light of buddha nature.

We can also think of our mind's basic goodness as a perfect, beautiful, white garment that has become stained by the mud of afflictive emotions. Those stains, the mud that cakes the white cloth, are not actually part of the cloth itself and can therefore be removed with enough effort of washing. Just so, the negative afflictive emotions that stain our basic goodness are not actually part of our mind itself. Therefore they too can be removed with enough disciplined effort and diligence. The work that must be done, the washing to remove the mind's stains that obscure our basic goodness, is shamatha meditation.

We can apply ourselves to performing all sorts of tantric methods, such as sadhana practices, to try to remove the stains of negative karma. However, without the basic discipline of mind that comes with the practice of shamatha, those tantric practices will not have the power to effect the change we need to wash the stains from our basic goodness, to clear away the clouds that obscure the full brilliance of our buddha nature. There are a very few great beings who, due to an accumulation of merit and sharpening of faculties from the practice of previous lifetimes, may be able to step immediately onto the tantric path with great results. However, most of us must first tame our minds so that the higher, tantric techniques can be integrated into our practice with greater effect.

8. Vipashyana and Mahamudra

HAVING GAINED some experience applying antidotes to overcome our obstacles and thus having attained some stability in calm abiding meditation, we are prepared to look more deeply into the nature of our mind.

We must analyze the nature of our mind in order to practice vipashyana meditation. *Vipashyana* means "insight," seeing in a way that you have never seen before. Vipashyana is the perfect insight that leads us not only to knowledge but also to profound realization of the nature of ultimate reality by focusing on and analyzing mind itself.

Most practitioners begin by engaging in shamatha meditation. As their advancement in shamatha progresses, deeper and deeper states of tranquility are attained. They then begin to have experiences of vipashyana, that profound and penetrating insight that comes as a result of shamatha practice. Eventually shamatha and vipashyana become inseparable, at which point vipashyana is no longer just a result of practice, but an intentional practice in itself. It is then that the practitioner moves ever more quickly toward the perfection of the meditative state of samadhi.

There are those fortunate ones who have particularly sharp or even uncanny faculties; they have an unusual aptitude for meditation practice. These seemingly inexplicable abilities for meditation are simply due to an accumulation of good karma, and therefore great merit. This is an indication that good deeds and extensive practice make up a good portion of these practitioners' more recent previous incarnations. These very rare, fortunate few are able to immediately experience a state of vipashyana without expending much time or effort toward shamatha practice at all. However, for most of us who are on the dharma path in this lifetime, extensive cultivation of our shamatha practice is necessary before we even begin to see the first blooming of the flowers of vipashyana experiences.

The perfection of vipashyana meditation is indeed like the blooming of a flower; that flower cannot bloom if we do not first cultivate the seed, which is the perfection of shamatha meditation. Once we see the blossoms of the initial vipashyana experiences, it is only a matter of time before those flowers become the true fruits: consistent sessions of penetrating insight into the nature of mind and reality that are the intentional practice of vipashyana.

Vipashyana practice is part of what is done in the three-year retreat. In order to practice in this way, we direct attention to and observe the qualities and attributes of the mind itself. In order to meditate on mind, the cultivation of mental tranquility is critical so that the mind is more easily controlled and one-pointedly focused, rather than distracted by various conceptions, or fabrications. This is why developing significant skill in shamatha meditation is such an important prerequisite to vipashyana. It is also very helpful to be in a proper setting or environment. This is the importance of the retreat setting, where we are free from everyday distractions and can focus on the nature of mind in a calm and open way.

VIPASHYANA AND THE CHARACTERISTICS OF MIND

Lord Gampopa taught that the way we should approach vipashyana meditation is to look at mind itself and analyze it, trying to understand what it is, what its defining characteristics are, what it is made of, and so forth. He spoke of different ways to investigate the mind:

- ▸ First of all, what is the substance, the entity, of mind?
- ▸ Second, what is its nature?
- ▸ Third, what are its defining characteristics?

When we analyze these questions they would seem to be leading us down different tracks of thought because of their different wording and specificity. However, the more we explore mind in an attempt to find answers to these questions, the clearer it becomes that all three eventually lead us to one simple yet unimaginably profound answer. This answer has three parts. First, the mind can be described as possessing luminous clarity. Second, the mind can be said to be unobstructed and spacious. Third, the mind is empty of inherent existence while possessing limitless possibility.

LUMINOUS CLARITY

When we look at the mind in its natural state, the first defining characteristic that we find is luminous clarity. Although "luminous clarity" might at first sound nebulous and esoteric, it has a very specific connotation in the context of meditation, specifically when meditating on the mind. Saying that the mind is luminous indicates that the mind possesses a quality of light. Because there is this quality of light, we are able to see, observe, and interpret phenomena as they arise, abide, and cease. The luminous mind also possesses the attribute of clarity; phenomena are not veiled or covered, but rather appear clearly and vividly.

If we think of the mind as being like a room, we could say that luminosity indicates that there is a bright light on in the room by which we are able to see its contents, the appearance of phenomena. We could also say that clarity indicates that the air in the room is clear, that there is an absence of anything like smoke or fog that would keep us from observing the contents of the room, i.e., those same phenomena. The distinction here is that both luminosity and clarity must be present for us to be able to see and observe; it is only because mind possesses luminous clarity that we are able to experience phenomena as they appear to us.

Many would exclaim that for those of us who have yet to attain liberation, the mind seems to be terribly obscured, both dark and cloudy, in direct contradiction of our description of the mind as being luminous and clear. It is critical to understand that luminous clarity is a description of the mind in its natural state, when mind is refined and unburdened by the kleshas and samskaras of karma. These obscurations are what cause us to perceive the mind as dark and cloudy rather than luminous and clear. It is only our confused and ignorant state of mind that causes us to experience reality from a view that lacks in clarity and luminosity; it is the obscurations that are dark and cloudy, not the mind itself. When we meditators engage in sufficient dharma practice to begin shedding these veils of obscuration that cloud and darken the mind, then we also begin to experience a view that is more and more luminous and clear. It is then that the perfection of shamatha and vipashyana can lead us into a state of mind that is so refined that we finally see what it is like to truly experience the luminous clarity of the mind in its natural state. This in turn brings us to a state that is much closer to liberation and enlightenment, which become possible with the perfection of vipashyana.

Unobstructed Spaciousness

When we engage in meditation on the nature of mind in its natural state, the second quality or characteristic of mind that we find is unobstructed spaciousness. This means that the space within which the mind operates is infinite, or limitless. There are no boundaries to the mind and therefore the mind can never be filled; our mind never runs out of room for more appearances to arise. Also, that space is unobstructed, meaning that there is nothing within the space of the mind that would keep the mind from moving about freely. It is because of this quality of spaciousness that appearances are capable of arising and then being observed and interpreted.

To better explain the characteristic of unobstructed spaciousness, we can return to our analogy of the mind as a room. We have already established that, due to the nature of mind being luminous and clear, the mind is like a room within which we are able to see because the light is on and the air is clear. But light and clarity are not enough to explain the appearance of phenomena. Obviously there must be space within the room for those appearances to arise, but that space must also be unobstructed; there must be sufficient space for an infinite number of appearances to arise. If this were not the case, eventually relative reality would "fill up," and no more appearances could arise! For this very reason, our analogy of the mind as a room falls quite short of reality, for the mind is so spacious that it is larger than any room we can imagine within relative reality.

The room of the mind in its natural state is so large that there are no walls that can be found to block movement within the mind. Because the room of our mind is infinitely spacious, there is no need for windows or doors, and therefore there is no way to lock the mind into a particular confine. Similarly, there are no limits on how high or low we can move within the room of the mind, so we could also say that there is no ceiling or floor. It is a room so large that it can never be filled up: there is always space for more phenomena to arise. The space within this room is also unobstructed, meaning that no matter how large or how many phenomena appear within the mind, they are not able to impede the mind's movement.

Many would hear this explanation of the unobstructed spaciousness of mind and exclaim that it is not true, that their experience of reality is made up of profound feelings of bondage and claustrophobia. Many can point to obvious examples of limitations, such as the imprisonment and enslavement that countless humans have experienced. At a more subtle level, we oftentimes experience the chains of afflictive emotion such as boredom, which can make us feel as though we are locked down mentally if not physically. At an even subtler level, we could say that we are bound by the chains of samsara that even further restrict our ability to move freely through the unobstructed space of ultimate reality.

However, all of these apparent limitations to unobstructed spaciousness are merely fabrications of the conceptual mind that are due to profound ignorance and confusion. This is why the perfection of shamatha and vipashyana are so critical to liberation and the experience of enlightenment. When we learn to meditate on the nature of mind itself and fully realize the nature of mind as being unobstructed space, then there is nothing that can restrict the movement of our minds. We experience a limitlessness that is unimaginable in our current, deluded state of mind of hopes and fears, of false dualities. We can then truly experience being freed of all boundaries, whether physical imprisonment, the bondage of afflictive emotion, or the chains of the cycle of rebirth and suffering that is samsara. When we finally experience full realization of unobstructed spaciousness, the bliss of nirvana is realized as well. This is the perfection of shamatha and vipashyana.

It is this unobstructed spaciousness that allows for the mind to reincarnate. Conversely, if we believe in reincarnation, then we also already have some notion of unobstructed spaciousness. By definition, unobstructed spaciousness as a quality of mind indicates that the mind is never truly bound or blocked in any way. The mind is therefore inherently independent of the physical body. One way to express this idea is the simple statement "I have a body, but I am not my body." Although we usually feel quite bound to our bodies, death has a very convincing way of showing us that we are not really locked in our bodies. We move into our body and remain there for a lifetime. When viewed from the infinite expanse of beginningless and endless time, that one lifetime is really quite short. Our mind has moved from body to body over countless lives, and will continue to do so until we have reached enlightenment and left the cycle of birth, death, and rebirth that characterizes samsara.

It is the unobstructed spaciousness of the mind in its natural state that allows this process to occur at all. When, through the cycle of samsara, we are born into this world as a human being, it is only our own ignorance and confusion that cause us to believe that we are bound to the body that we have come to inhabit. We are so confused that we sometimes even come to believe that we are not just trapped in that body, but that we *are* that body. We are unable to differentiate between our body and our mind, and our body becomes an integral part of our identity. However, the process of reincarnation—the cyclical birth, death, and rebirth that is samsara—should be an incredibly convincing illustration of just how false this "body as self" view really is. Rather than being our body, we inhabit many, even infinite bodies over the course of our time in samsara. Changing bodies is not much different than changing clothes, albeit more traumatic due to the fact that we are typically far more attached to our bodies than we are to any of our clothing.

EMPTINESS AND LIMITLESS POSSIBILITY

When studying the nature of mind, the one subject that comes up most frequently and that seems to get the most attention among practitioners of insight meditation, is this quality of mind that is most commonly described as emptiness of inherent existence, which tends to get shortened to "emptiness." Another way that some describe this same quality is to say the mind possesses limitless possibility for transformation. There is nothing perceived by the mind that is permanent, changeless, or independently existent. Everything that the mind perceives is a dependently arisen phenomenon that can cease to appear just as easily as it seemed to appear within the mind. No matter how hard we try or how far back we look, there is always something that came before that provided the causes and conditions for the arising of a particular phenomenon.

Take your car, for example. It is easy to see how the car is dependently arisen: it is a collection of parts assembled by one or more people or even robots in a factory. If any one of those parts was missing, or if any one of the people or machines failed to correctly execute their task, the car would not work properly or even at all. However, we tend to think of our car as being quite solid and real. We tend to think that our car truly exists. But what if we took one tire off of the car? If someone asked us if we own a car, we would still say yes, even if it was just missing one tire. If we take this example to its logical extreme and eventually strip the car of all parts but the engine, would we still have a car? Most would say no, certainly not, we have a car engine. But, at what point did the car stop being a car and become component parts instead? This can go even further: the parts are all made of materials such as glass, plastic, and metal. In our modern world we know full well that these too can be broken down into smaller parts such as simpler chemical compounds, base elements, and further into subatomic particles such as protons, neutrons, and electrons, and even smaller particles like quarks. It seems that every time we turn around, physics has discovered yet a smaller foundational particle upon which your car is eventually built! So how existent is your car after all?

The same is true of all phenomena arising. We can attempt to find a singular, foundational event from which all things ultimately arise, yet there is none. In fact, if there were, no arising could ever take place. The relative universe would be changeless because there would be no ability for any event to occur or thing to appear, because both of those things require change at some level no matter how subtle. Therefore we can say with confidence that not only is the mind empty of inherent existence, but also that because of that emptiness, the mind possesses limitless possibility for change and transformation.

An important distinction to be made here is the difference between the Buddhist view of emptiness and the rather unsavory view that is nihilism. Nihilism is the belief that nothing exists, that all phenomena are void, and that no appearances exist. Unfortunately, this nihilistic view of the relative universe also has a logical extreme: that nothing matters, that there is no right or wrong, and that beings can act in any way, no matter how negative, without any sort of consequences, karmic or otherwise. But this is clearly not the case. I can see phenomena arise; I can describe the appearances that come into my mind. As Buddhists we are not making the claim that nothing exists in the sense that all phenomena are void or nonexistent. Instead we are merely observing that phenomena are not truly and inherently existent either; that there are in fact appearances that come about due to causes and conditions. Because these appearances are dependent upon those causes and conditions, they are therefore capable of disappearing as easily as they appeared. It is not so much that things do not exist, but that they do not exist independently of other things. Because of this interdependent relationship between all phenomena, there is actually a lot less solidity and much more fluidity than we might normally perceive within superficial, relative reality. The important distinction to be made here is that although Buddhists are confident in the view of emptiness and limitless possibility within relative reality, we can also remain confident in the laws of karmic cause and effect as well as the existence of suffering within the bounds of samsara. Thus, we do not fall into a nihilistic downward spiral of amoral narcissism.

One of the most exciting implications of this view of the universe is that once we have truly realized the ultimate nature of our own mind, we also therefore realize the ultimate nature of all phenomena because these have arisen within the mind. This ultimate view of relative reality is what allows the meditator who has perfected shamatha and vipashyana to come to rest in a state of true samadhi that is equivalent to omniscience, a place of transcendent awareness of all phenomena. We in the modern world may think that we know a great many things and that we have come so far in our understanding of our universe. This is true in the sense that we have done an excellent job of mapping out a good portion of relative reality. But, because as a species, humans have done really very little to know the nature of our own minds, we really don't know that much at all. Not knowing the nature of our own minds, we know very little about the nature of our own existence. However, once we do come to know the nature of our minds, we will no longer be so dependent upon the knowledge of the mundane, phenomenal world which we currently spend so much time and energy studying. Not knowing our mind, we know nothing; knowing our mind, we know everything.

NATURE OF MIND AND VIPASHYANA

This is my heartfelt advice to genuine practitioners. Here, I will explain how to contemplate the nature of mind itself as simply as possible without compromising the integrity of these profound instructions. The practice of shamatha and vipashyana must be uncontrived and unmanipulated. It does no good to disturb or otherwise influence the mind, for this only sends ripples of thoughts and fabrications across the surface of our mind stream. Rather, the mind should be observed, explored, and contemplated while in its natural state of tranquility and calm abiding.

When we reach this state of calm abiding, we should not grasp on to the experience and attempt to guide it, or even make the experience into some fabrication or construction more familiar to our conceptual minds' usual modality of experience. We should instead take a metaphorical step back and observe from an unattached state, thereby developing an even calmer and more tranquil witness consciousness. When the mind is seen to be scattered or unclear, know that this is shamatha and vipashyana itself. By seeing the mind's scattered state or lack of clarity, we are already engaging in a practice of observing the mind. It is the mind that possesses the qualities of being scattered and unclear and, as our consciousness witnesses those qualities, the mind then begins to meditate on mind itself. In brief, the meditator must rest the mind in a calm and tranquil state of transcendent awareness that is free from conceptual fabrication and distractions of discursive thoughts.

The mind must rest in its natural state yet maintain clarity and focus. This state can be compared to the experience of lying in the grass, looking up, and observing a clear blue sky upon which we are focused one-pointedly. A bird may fly by, entering the field of our vision, crossing the clear blue sky above us, and then flying on and thereby leaving the field of vision. However, it is possible that, although our mind notices the appearance and disappearance of the bird at some superficial level, at no point does our mind actually wander from the clear blue sky upon which we are so intently focused. This is how we must meditate. The mind in its natural state is that clear blue sky, and the bird is a thought that arises, abides for a moment, and then dissipates on its own, self-liberated. Although we are aware of the bird, we do not allow the mind to engage with the bird.

The mind and the bird do not interact in any way, and thus neither has any effect on the other. Just so, if we do not engage with a thought as it arises, there can be no chain of discursive thoughts that result from that engagement. Therefore, there will also be no interaction with thoughts to produce obstacles to one-pointed meditation. The thought has no effect on the mind; the mind has no effect on the thought.

We do not need tools to find the mind. We do not need to go anywhere to search for it. We do not need to dig down to unearth the mind; we do not need a map to reveal its location, nor must we travel by car, airplane, or any other vehicle in order to arrive at an observation of the mind. Our body and mind are, for the time being, inseparable; they will not part ways until the very end of our life at the precise moment of our death.

EMOTIONS AND VIPASHYANA

When our mind experiences moments of afflictive emotion, rather than see them as distracting obstructions in our path, we must use those emotions as fuel for our practice. Generally speaking, most practitioners either attach to and attempt to extend, or make permanent, any emotions that we label as positive. We also have the tendency to express our aversion to emotions that we identify as negative by avoiding them or attempting to eliminate their causes and conditions. However, rather than taking this habitual approach toward any afflictive emotion that arises in our minds, we can instead use it as fuel for our practice of shamatha and vipashyana by focusing on that experience of emotion and exploring its nature.

This makes perfect sense because, when we are afflicted by intense emotion, that emotion is very easy for us to focus upon and engage with at a very deep level. We can attempt to find an original, unsupported, and inherently existent cause or condition for the arising of this emotion. We can try to label its attributes: What size is it? What are its dimensions? What color is it? What does this emotion smell and taste like? When we fail to identify a concrete answer to any of these questions and explorations, we not only learn how to better focus the mind one-pointedly, we also receive reinforcement in the emptiness of phenomena. The added benefit of this type of practice is that, by resting for a moment in this certainty that the afflictive emotion is empty of inherent existence, the emotion is self-liberated and therefore no longer an affliction.

DUALITY AND VIPASHYANA

The ordinary practitioner may cultivate some small experience of tranquility and calm abiding through the practice of shamatha. However, it is only the advanced meditator who can use her experience and practice of deep states of vipashyana to dispel the false duality of subject and object. Normally, we separate the world into two categories that can be described by any of the following pairs: subject and object, "I" and "other," observer and observed, meditator and meditated, mind and phenomena, and many others.

For instance, we may see a tree and label it with the identifying word "tree," but then we also establish a state of separation between our self and the tree. We are making the confused assumption that these two things, the self and the tree, can exist independently of each other, that both observer and observed can abide and remain without the other. But this is terribly mistaken. Without something to observe, how could there be something identified as an observer? On the other hand, without the observer, how could there be something that is observed?

Observer and observed are dependent upon each other for their apparent existence; this is what we mean when we say that all phenomena are dependently arisen. We cannot find anything in our relative experience of reality that exists completely independently, without causes and conditions for its appearance in our mind. Hence, we must also come to the conclusion that, from an ultimate sense, because all phenomena are lacking inherent existence and there is no true separation of mind and phenomena, therefore mind itself is also lacking permanent, unchanging, and inherent existence.

PERSPECTIVE AND VIPASHYANA

Vipashyana deals directly with the mind itself. Once established in a stable and unshakable state of tranquility and calm abiding, we then begin the search for the mind and attempt to ascertain its location, qualities, and attributes. We must continue this process until absolute certainty is established that the mind neither has any location nor can it be described in ways that would allow us to believe that the mind is an object that can be found and possessed. This repeated search for mind and its description is a powerful and effective practice of shamatha and vipashyana all of its own. This process can be compared to a man who rides around on a donkey, leading four more donkeys behind him. He can look back at any time and count his four donkeys, but whenever he encounters someone on his path, he asks them, "Have you seen my fifth donkey?" They see the four donkeys behind him and say no, they haven't seen his fifth donkey.

But then someone asks the man, "How many donkeys do you have?" to which he replies, "I own a total of five donkeys—that's why I'm searching for my fifth!" What he has forgotten is that the fifth donkey is beneath him. The person tells him, "Sir, you are riding your fifth donkey!" It is the same way with our mind, but we are even closer to our mind than the man is to the donkey upon which he rides. Just as the man on the donkey searches for his donkey, our mind is what searches for the location and description of mind itself.

This illustrates just how confused our point of view becomes when we use the mind so frequently, every day of our lives. We get so caught up in the thoughts and ideas that run through our mind, so caught up in the appearances of external and internal phenomena, that we become forgetful of mind itself. Just as the rider needs a reminder from an objective passerby, so too we need our gurus to remind us of the existence of our own mind's nature.

HIGHEST PRACTICES AND VIPASHYANA

Obviously, the practice and perfection of shamatha and vipashyana require great patience and diligence. It is also critical that the practitioner possess confidence: confidence in the truth and power of the practices, confidence in oneself to carry out those practices, and complete confidence, or certainty, that those practices will bring the fulfillment and realization that the great sages experienced. We must bring all of these things—patience, diligence and confidence—into our practice of shamatha and vipashyana. In fact, we can also bring every moment and every experience into our meditation practice. As long as we always remain mindful and aware of our every experience, all the while never losing sight of the inseparability of mind from the appearances that we experience, then every experience becomes part of our shamatha and vipashyana.

The ultimate meditation practice, Mahamudra, the Great Seal, is none other than realizing the ultimate nature of mind itself. The foundation of Mahamudra practice is that the mind is free of any conceptual fabrications. Thus, in order to experience ultimate meditation, the mind must be observed and contemplated while left in its natural state, luminous and clear.

The ultimate path of practice, Madhyamaka, the Middle Way, is none other than realizing the ultimate nature of mind itself. The foundation of the Madhyamaka path is that the mind is inseparable from emptiness and limitless possibility. Thus, in order to experience the ultimate path, the mind must be viewed from the Middle Way. This means the mind is recognized as being neither void (which is the view of nihilism) nor existent and unchanging (the view of eternalism). Rather, there is a union of emptiness and appearance arising, a path of perfect purity that is the one taste of relative and ultimate reality, inseparable.

The ultimate fruition of practice, Dzogchen, the Great Perfection, is none other than realizing the ultimate nature of mind itself. The foundation of the Dzogchen fruition is that the mind is inseparable from unobstructed spaciousness; therefore mind is unbounded and unlimited. It is fundamentally impossible to chain or bind the mind. It is therefore an inherent quality of the mind that it has limitless ability to transcend and escape the suffering of samsara. This escape, this liberation, is the ultimate fruition.

9. Obstacles to Vipashyana and
Their Antidotes

W HAT FOLLOWS NEXT is my heartfelt advice regarding obstacles to vipashyana. Ultimately, as meditators, we must learn to completely avoid obstacles altogether; however, for most beginning and even intermediate meditators, avoiding obstacles is quite difficult. Instead, it is more likely that we will encounter these obstacles and then need to learn how to overcome them by facing them head-on. When we look directly at and into the core of our obstacles while remaining calm and tranquil, we can arrive at certain conclusions. First, we find that our obstacles are really just afflictive emotions, arising as a result of specific causes and conditions. Second, we can also see that those causes and conditions are also merely dependently arisen phenomena. Third, we begin to realize that, no matter how far back we look to try and find an original, self-arisen, and inherently existent cause from which our obstacle originated, there is none to be found.

Thus, our obstacles are empty of inherent existence and therefore self-liberated. It is important to maintain the focus and tranquility of deep and skillful shamatha meditation throughout the application of the antidote to obstacles, for only then can we continue on toward the perfection of vipashyana.

Infinite Thoughts and Vipashyana

One of the most common obstacles to vipashyana is the experience of becoming overwhelmed and confused by the infinite number of thoughts that can come to the surface of our mind stream when we attempt to focus one-pointedly. It is important to realize that, regardless of the fact that we may have reached some of the more advanced stages of meditation, those infinite thoughts will actually continue to surface. What changes as we advance is the level of skill with which we deal with that constant flow of thoughts. At first we begin to develop some skill with taming our minds by not only bringing the mind into focus but also keeping it focused by not engaging or interacting with thoughts. In this way, we stay focused by simply allowing thoughts to dissipate on their own, naturally, without exerting any effort to try to make them go away.

Thoughts arise, they abide for a moment, and then they disappear. As we gain more skill in vipashyana, we develop the transcendent awareness and penetrating insight that cultivates a profound sense of witness consciousness. This witness consciousness enables us to observe the thoughts themselves without getting caught up in discursive reflections that then overwhelm and confuse us. We can maintain a kind of metaphorical distance from which we observe and analyze as an unattached and objective witness. From this state of witness consciousness, we can begin to see the impermanent and even inherent emptiness of the thoughts that float through our mind and inspire afflictive emotions.

Eventually we reach a point where we have such skill that no thought, regardless of how disturbing, can interrupt or confuse our meditation session. It is important to maintain the focus and tranquility of deep and skillful shamatha meditation throughout the application of the antidote for the disturbance of infinite thoughts. This is the mark of a truly advanced vipashyana meditator.

HYPERSENSITIVITY AND VIPASHYANA

For meditators who have developed a certain degree of skill in shamatha, and even some skill in vipashyana, an obstacle that may arise is hypersensitivity. This happens to the meditator whose mind and emotions seem to swing quite easily from one extreme to the next. It is as if every time the winds of change blow through their lives (which inevitably happens), they are swept away by those winds. They go from happy and joyful to dark and depressed quite easily, many times even more easily than someone who does not meditate at all and is only rooted firmly in the mundane world. This is a profound obstacle to the perfection of vipashyana.

The only solution, once this sort of obstacle develops, is to recognize this hypersensitive, easily affected, and moody nature the moment it arises; and then, firmly refuse to indulge it. Become completely unwilling to entertain the mind's vacillations through so many states of afflictive emotion! Once there is a feeling of distance from this hypersensitivity, it becomes much less likely that hypersensitivity will be able to overcome the mind's calm and tranquil state. We can begin to observe and analyze that hypersensitivity in the same way that we would any other distracting thought or afflictive emotion.

One can apply the techniques mentioned before that will enable us to dismantle these obstacles and negative states of mind altogether, so that they lose their power to plague us. It is important to maintain the focus and tranquility of deep and skillful shamatha meditation throughout the application of the antidote for hypersensitivity. Then the meditator can continue to move forward once again toward the perfection of vipashyana.

Adversity and Vipashyana

One of the most common obstacles for practitioners of meditation is that of adversity, or negative experience. The most obvious of these is sickness. As soon as we become hurt or ill we tend to take time off from our practice, as though we are taking "sick days" from our dharma practice the same way that we would take time off from work when we become ill. Many people believe that if they cannot give their best meditative effort due to injury or disease, then they should make no effort at all, and rest instead. But disease is not the only negative experience that seems to keep students away from their practice. When funds are short and they are worried about providing themselves, or even their families, with food and shelter, practice suffers.

When we fight with our spouse or boss, practice suffers. When our home is damaged in a storm or we are robbed, or when we are simply in a bad mood, practice suffers. However, this makes no sense; it is really just another form of procrastination. If we only practice when our situation is just right, we would hardly ever have the "right" time for meditation. In fact, there are many reasons why adverse circumstances actually provide us with the perfect time for meditation practice. Negative experiences provide us with a very clear view of the inherent suffering of samsara, and, therefore, the need to practice dharma so that we may find a real solution for our suffering.

The sufferings we experience from negative situations are actually just the results of negative karma coming to fruition. Thus, what better way to shorten our experience of the sufferings from negative karma than to accumulate the merit from positive karma by engaging in meditation practice? When we are in the midst of suffering due to the stormy waves of samsara, nothing gives us relief like time spent in the tranquility and calm abiding of shamatha meditation. In fact, when one begins to taste the penetrating insight of vipashyana, it is so much more likely that one will quickly find the way out of those stormy seas.

Really, it is no large feat to meditate and maintain focus when everything in our lives is going as we would like. It is actually the advanced meditator who is able to remain focused and calm when obstacles such as negative experiences arise. We must cultivate the discipline to return to meditation practice day after day, regardless of how we feel on a daily basis. Then, consistent practice becomes second nature and requires much less effort to begin each day.

It is important to mention at this point that it is not just negative experiences that can become obstacles to practice. Long stretches of time full of positive experiences and enjoyment of the mundane world can also pose similar obstacles to meditation if the meditator does not remain vigilant toward the temptations of samsara. When life is going particularly well, practitioners tend to forget the truth of suffering that brought them to their practice to begin with. They get caught up in enjoyment of the temporary and illusory nature of the pleasures of samsara. Fortunately, as soon as those pleasures fade or new sufferings enter their lives, those same students are generally quick to return to their practice once they realize that they've given up the one thing that could release them from their sufferings: dharma practice. However, it would be far better if these students could remain diligent in their effort of practice regardless of their personal situation, whether good or bad.

Self-Esteem and Vipashyana

Another common obstacle for beginning and even intermediate meditators is negative self-esteem, also called negative self-image. When we have a negative view of ourselves, our potential, and our abilities, we tend to see much less progression in our practice. This is basically another form of doubt or skepticism. Although we may have faith in the dharma and its practice, we have no faith in our own abilities to carry out that practice.

While we may have faith in the buddhas, bodhisattvas, great sages, and other realized beings that came before us, we have no faith in the fact that they were once just like us and that, therefore, we too can attain their great state if we practice in the way that they did. When self-image is particularly negative we can spend all of our time crying, pouting, and throwing self-indulgent fits of depression and self-pity rather than engaging in the very practice that could lift us up and out of our pathetic state. When negative self-esteem becomes an obstacle to practice, the antidote is quite simple: lighten up. Focus for a time on images in the mind that make you feel happy and strong. Open the eyes wide and lift the head up to open the heart and mind, to feel lighter and brighter. Don't let the weight of the sufferings of the world weigh you down. Don't even let the weight of being such a serious practitioner weigh so heavily upon your mind.

Always remember that every enlightened being once experienced doubts and skepticism, suffering and other negativities, that impeded their progress as well. Just like them, if you continue to practice with a lighter heart, then eventually your faith in yourself and your faith in the dharma will banish the obstacles of dark thoughts from low self-esteem.

COMPLICATION AND VIPASHYANA

A common obstacle for meditators striving for vipashyana is overcomplicating vipashyana practice; they complain that it is simply too difficult to meditate on the nature of mind. They complain that, although they could accomplish anything else in the world to which they put their mind, nothing is more difficult than recognizing the true nature of their own mind. This view is merely a sign or symptom that they do not truly understand vipashyana meditation. This profound difficulty that they perceive only seems true because they have not received the proper instructions to execute the practice; they have yet to connect properly, for if they were properly connected they would realize that it is not difficult at all.

To observe the nature of our own mind is really quite simple. Our mind is always with us no matter where we travel; it cannot be purchased, it cannot be lost, nor is it constructed or made. When we search, construct, or look for something that can be bought, it is the mind itself that is doing those things. It is the mind that labels and interprets as we search and construct. When we cease these fabricated activities of mind and simply rest and observe without attachment, it is the nature of mind itself that enables us to engage in that very act of observation. It is in that moment of rest and observation that we can begin to realize the nature of mind and enter a state of vipashyana.

UNCREATED MIND AND VIPASHYANA

Yet another obstacle to vipashyana meditation is the mistaken notion that the mind could come to an end or be lost in some way. Is essential to have confidence that the mind is uncreated and therefore cannot be destroyed. Since beginningless time, the mind has been appearing in some form or another, and will not disappear at any point in the unending future. People sometimes refer to "losing their mind," but it is important to realize that this is merely a saying, a colloquial expression. The mind can be neither lost nor found. Saying that you have lost your mind is an indication that you are using it to observe and analyze the current state of your mind. It is quite correct, however, to say that you have lost awareness, presence, or perspective. Generally what we mean when we say that we have lost our minds is that we have experienced a moment of profound confusion.

But, the very fact that we are able to observe the mind and then identify that confusion is incontrovertible proof that we still have our mind and that it still retains some degree of transcendent awareness. When we realize that the mind is forever and always with us and capable of observation and description, then we also realize our own ability to explore and identify the true nature of mind and to continue toward the perfection of vipashyana.

HOPES, FEARS, AND VIPASHYANA

Many students experience profound difficulties in learning to focus the mind one-pointedly, opening the mind in a way that is spacious and unobstructed, and realizing the luminous and limitless possibility of mind itself. These students become disappointed or discouraged when they read about these things but then have no profound realizations or mind-blowing experiences the first time they sit down to meditate.

These hopes of attainments and fears of failure represent some of the most substantial obstacles on the path toward liberation. The Buddha Shakyamuni meditated ceaselessly for six years to attain enlightenment, so it is ridiculous to think that an ordinary beginning meditator would have meaningful realizations and experiences by practicing for several minutes or even a few hours each day. Although we have found the precious dharma and begun a practice, it is crucial to remember that we still carry with us the defilements of negative karma built up over countless lives since begin-ningless time.

If we are to have the meditation experiences of a buddha, if we are to have the realizations of a buddha, if we are to become a buddha, then we must cleanse ourselves of defilements so that we become pure and stainless like a buddha. We must dig out the very roots of afflictive emotion and remove the very seeds of passion, aggression, and ignorance.

These defilements are like clouds that block the sunlight of our poten-tial for buddhahood; our negative karma blocks the luminosity of our own basic goodness, or buddha nature. We must live a life of positivity and virtue in accordance with the dharma in addition to engaging in the profound practice of meditation. By living virtuously we accumulate positive karma or merit, which causes our basic goodness to shine brighter.

By engaging in meditation practice we purify those defilements that cloud or obscure what light comes from our buddha nature. Do not lose heart in thinking that your light is too dim and your defilements too thick. The fact that you have found the dharma is proof that your defilements are not so powerful and that they can be overcome. Your desire to engage in meditation practice is proof that your tendency toward basic goodness is already beginning to light the path out of darkness and toward liberation. When we continue to live and practice in accordance with the dharma, we can slowly but surely overcome the obstacles of our own defilements and continue toward the perfection of vipashyana.

Skepticism and Vipashyana

There is a specific type of doubt, or skepticism, which creates a great obstacle to the practice of vipashyana. Many meditators, upon beginning a practice of observing the nature of mind itself, immediately question the validity of such a practice and the experiences that result from it. As they attempt to engage in practice, they experience skepticism about the validity of this type of practice. They are unsure of their moments of realization of the nature of mind. They are plagued with doubts about their own abilities to properly execute the instructions for meditating on the nature of mind. This is not practicing meditation! It is practicing doubt! These meditators get better and better at doubt and skepticism instead of getting better at resting the mind in one-pointed contemplation of the nature of mind itself.

To overcome this obstacle, this particular type of doubt, we must put aside all doubts. When we meditate, we should not contemplate, entertain, or otherwise dwell on doubts and skepticism! When we are engaged in a meditation session, we must let our one-pointed concentration fill the mind so thoroughly that there is no room left for doubt. Later, when we are off the cushion and operating in the relative, phenomenal world, we can explore our questions and doubts. Entertaining your skepticism with your internal debates can help you come to a greater place of surety and confidence in the truth of dharma and meditation practice. However, when on the cushion and engaged in a session of meditation on the nature of mind, let no doubt linger in your mind stream. When you can do that, then you will move much more quickly toward the perfection of vipashyana meditation.

PREOCCUPATIONS AND VIPASHYANA

One of the most common obstacles faced by meditators practicing shamatha and vipashyana is preoccupation with the material world. The number of material distractions available to the mind is infinite; the opportunities to wander from the intended state of focus are limitless. Many sit and think of the material possessions they would like to acquire, or dwell on the things they already possess that they enjoy and appreciate; or they think about those possessions with which they are dissatisfied and which they would like to fix or replace. They sit and explore their fear that they may lose the things they enjoy and then engage in attempts to create ways to protect themselves from this loss.

Their minds wander to other places within the material world, whether a mountain they would like to visit, a beach that they are fond of and to which they would like to return, or a favorite restaurant where they would like to be eating. The list of places they would rather be, other than on their cushion, is just as infinite as the list of possessions that they could own. These types of sidetracks from our true path of practice can completely negate our shamatha meditation. Just because we sit in the same spot day after day with our legs crossed does not mean that we are meditating. If our object of focus constantly shifts from one material and mundane thing to the next, we are merely daydreaming, not meditating. Daydreaming is a serious obstacle to meditation because it shows us that as meditators we are still very attached to the pleasures of samsara as the sources of happiness and refuge from suffering.

To overcome this type of obstacle, we would do well to once again come back to contemplating the four noble truths until the certainty arises that the mundane world has no lasting material pleasures, that the only path away from suffering and toward liberation is the practice of the dharma. It is important to mention at this point that it is normal, particularly in the beginning stages of meditation practice, for the mind to wander from the chosen object of meditative focus. However, we can only consider the meditation session successful if the meditator realizes that the mind has wandered and brings it back to the original object of focus. Over time, these wanderings should occur less and less often, until eventually the meditator can focus one-pointedly for as long as she chooses. It is at this point that the perfection of shamatha is reached and experiences of penetrating insight and transcendent awareness will move the meditator closer and closer toward the perfection of vipashyana.

ENTERTAINMENT AND VIPASHYANA

Many practitioners who attempt to meditate on the nature of mind encounter obstacles by getting caught up in observing the phenomena that arise, abide, and disappear within the mind. There is an important distinction to be made here. We do begin to explore the inherent emptiness of phenomenal appearances by observing their appearance and disappearance within the mind. However, obstacles arise when a meditator gets caught up in this practice to the point that he no longer seeks the nature of mind at all, but instead stands by and observes these appearances one after the other as though simply watching a movie or television show within the mind.

This is not transcendent awareness. This is merely another source of entertainment by daydreaming, for the appearances will never cease if we continue to give them our energy and attention. One appearance gives rise to the next, on and on, in an infinite string of dependently arisen phenomena. If we seek to meditate on the nature of mind, we must not give these appearances our attention and therefore our energy. It is normal for phenomena to arise within the mind when we are attempting to meditate on the nature of mind itself. But know that, if we stay focused while maintaining the transcendent awareness of witness consciousness as we observe and explore the nature of mind, then those phenomenal thoughts and appearances will disappear just as naturally and easily as they appeared. Over time, whatever phenomena should arise within the mind will disturb our focus on the nature of mind less and less. Eventually, we become able to remain completely undisturbed by the appearance of any and all phenomena. Appearances are self-liberated and we are free to be completely and perfectly absorbed in the nature of our own mind, moving us quickly toward the perfection of vipashyana.

Chasing Thoughts and Vipashyana

Some meditators experience a type of obstacle that causes them to actually chase after thoughts and appearances that have arisen and then dissipated. This is most commonly seen in meditators who have experienced a brief appearance within the mind that gives them a pleasurable feeling. When that thought dissipates, they chase after it as though they are trying to track it down so that they may observe it again. However, it is quite possible, even common, that someone would race after a thought that gives them feelings that are not pleasurable at all.

Remember how often you have been emotionally stuck, dwelling on one thought or appearance of something that causes you pain or suffering in some way. We may say that we are in a bad mood, or even depressed; however, what is a mood but one particular thought repeated over and over again? What is depression but one negative view repeated over and over, a negative view from which we cannot escape? Whether pleasurable or painful, when we chase after a thought that has disappeared, we get caught by this obstacle of constantly trying to revisit our thoughts. Trying to track down a thought that has disappeared is just as ridiculous as trying to track down a bird that, although it was in our field of vision for a moment, has now flown on and out of sight.

Flying birds leave no tracks or traces for us to follow, and a thought that has disappeared from our mind stream is no different. We must learn to let thoughts that have disappeared stay that way; we must recognize that they are impermanent, and remain focused on our one-pointed exploration of the nature, rather than the contents, of our own minds. When a thought disappears, remain focused on the fact that the one who noticed the disappearance is the mind, and then return to watching the watcher. When we learn to use the mind to explore the mind, we observe the observer. We become adept at witnessing our own consciousness, and the perfection of vipashyana is ours in which to rest, tranquil and calmly abiding.

DEDICATION OF MERIT

Namo Buddhaya!
Namo Dharmhaya!
Namo Sanghaya!

Having spent my entire life
Listening, contemplating, and meditating upon the dharma,
Whatever merit I have accumulated
I dedicate to the enlightenment of all beings.
Without exception, may they attain omniscience!

Since beginningless time
Negative karma has been the obstacle of liberation.
Fear is the enemy of freedom!
Fear of the stormy waves of birth, old age, sickness, and death,
Fear of the ocean of samsara,
The chains of fear keep beings imprisoned in the cycle of suffering.
By the power of this dedication, may I free all beings from their
    bondage in samsara.

Just as the Bodhisattva Manjushri became dedicated,
And likewise Samantabhadra accomplished the same,
So too, by following their example,
May I attain omniscience.
Those practitioners like myself,
And all others who come into contact with this book,
May they attain the Tathagata's omniscience.

May I dedicate this book to the benefit of all readers,
That this book be the seed,
The cause of their success on the journey toward their ultimate goal.
By the planting of the seeds of virtuous action,
Gathered from the three times, past, present, and future,
Sown and cultivated in a single place,
May this book be the cause of the fruition of enlightenment.

I dedicate this writing to all beings equally, without exception.
May all who read these words be perfected by the accumulation of wisdom
and merit.

May enlightenment be achieved!
Sarva mangalam!

AUTOBIOGRAPHICAL AFTERWORD
SANSKRIT UNIVERSITY AND THREE-YEAR RETREAT

THE MOST SERIOUS and intense period of my formal education began when I was about seventeen. It was then that I entered the nine years of training toward my acharya degree at Sanskrit University. The university is located in the Uttar Pradesh region of India. Hostels for the university were some seven miles away in Sarnath. I arrived in the middle of the night, and there was no one to be found. Sarnath is also the site of the famed Deer Park, where Buddha Shakyamuni completed the first turning of the wheel of dharma, so I didn't really mind having a little extra time to take in the energy of this special place. I circumambulated and did prostrations at the Great Stupa. A stupa is a monument representing the heart of the Buddha. The great dharma king Ashoka built this particular stupa. I was overcome

SANSKRIT UNIVERSITY CLASS. INSET: LAMA DUDJOM DORJEE.
PHOTOGRAPH COURTESY OF THE AUTHOR.

with a deep tranquility and, in that moment, in the solitude of that holy and auspicious place, I knew in my heart that I would find success at Sanskrit University.

Eventually the sun began to rise and I made my way to the Kagyu student hostel where dozens of young students, including the Kagyu abbot, were having some breakfast and tea. Without hesitation, I walked directly but respectfully to the abbot and handed him a letter from the Venerable Tharchen Rinpoche, the Kagyu ambassador to the Tibetan Government-in-Exile in Dharamsala. The abbot, the Venerable Khenpo Yeshe Chodar, calmly took a moment to read the letter. When he had finished, he said, "According to this letter, you're pretty special. But we'll see about that."

Immediately he ordered one of the students to bring in some chalk and a chalkboard. They put the chalk in my hand and right there on the spot the Khenpo asked me to write some Buddhist verses. The abbot recited the verses and I was to transcribe them onto the blackboard. Apparently, I did okay because the students in the room began to clap. There was one face in the crowd of students I recognized as a member of my clan. His name was Tsondu Singhe. He remembered me too, and he stood up and called out, "If he can't make it, none of us can!" The abbot, however, didn't seem so easily convinced. "We'll see," was all that he said. But the important thing was that I was accepted as a Kagyu student under Khenpo's charge.

I immediately began to study Sanskrit, Hindi, and Tibetan, as well as to memorize the more important root texts from the canon of Buddhist philosophy. These were challenging subjects that required serious focus, and I quickly adjusted to a life of minimal comforts and distractions in which the greatest excitements were the fruits of knowledge and wisdom that came from diligent study. We woke at four a.m., with only the white stars of dawn to greet us as we walked out to catch the free bus that would transport us from the hostel where we slept to the university itself. If we happened to miss the bus, it was a long hike; even with great effort we weren't likely to make it to class that day. We could always take the next bus but would be required to pay, which no student could really afford. At least in these early hours of the morning, the oppressive daytime heat was not yet upon us. In the months of June, July, and August, by midday, the earth felt baked in the heat of the Indian sun. There was no air conditioning in any of the hostels, and I think I could have cooked my meals on the hot ground had I wanted to. Even at night the air was thick and humid. It was so hot that I slept on the hostel's roof in the open air, lying safely under a mosquito net. Mosquitoes buzzed and sang all night, anxious to sample me for a midnight snack.

I lived on about fifty rupees a month, which I received through a scholarship offered by the Indian government. In order to continually qualify for this scholarship, I had to pass all of the exams that were given twice a year. At that time, fifty rupees were equivalent to about three dollars. I had no choice but to create a life of few unnecessary expenses and I did manage to live nine years on that modest stipend. Let me be clear about the tests that had to be passed: they were grueling. Every six months, we were required to go before a jury panel and demonstrate our knowledge of specific root texts from the Madhyamaka, the Vinaya Sutra, the Abhidharma, the Prajnaparamita sutras, as well as many others. At the beginning of each semester we would be made aware of which chapters we would be expected to learn and by the end of the semester we were expected to have them completely memorized. By the end of the six years of study required to attain the shastra degree (the equivalent of the Western bachelor's degree), we were expected to have every word of every root text completely memorized; all of this memorization was in addition to the tests we were given in our regular classes.

At the end of my undergraduate years, the ever-important final exams loomed. I, like all of my classmates, wanted to continue studying toward my acharya degree after I completed my shastra degree. Before that could happen, though, I needed to qualify by passing the final exams. Even though I didn't believe I was the smartest in my class, I promised myself I would work harder than ever and studied many hours. Often, I would study all through the night, stopping only when the morning gong sounded to begin the next day with our predawn bus ride.

On exam day the tension was palpable—there was so much riding on it for all of us. There were approximately forty students who had begun the training toward their shastra degree, and some had not made it through all six years. They represented all four of the major lineages of Tibetan Buddhism. One of my classmates was so nervous that he was having trouble reading his exam. It seemed he suddenly couldn't read Tibetan anymore, until he realized that he had his test upside down! I had never cheated, and always let my effort earn what it may. Now, there was nothing left to do but wait for the results.

At this same time, with three more years remaining to earn my acharya degree, Sanskrit University began to experience some financial turmoil. Many scholarships, including mine, were in danger of being lost. School administrators consulted His Holiness the Dalai Lama, as well as Indian officials, for a solution to the crisis. In the meantime, many of us protested in hopes that we could prevent our scholarships from being eliminated. This period of limbo lasted about six months, during which time our stipends were suspended. The stipend was my only source of income, so I certainly never would have survived those six months without some outside help. I wrote to my foster father, Jean Claude, explaining my predicament. Without any hesitation he simply asked "How much do you need?" He became my sponsor and adopted me as if I were his own son. Through his generosity I was able to weather that shaky period at the university, and I have always been deeply grateful for that.

Finally, at the end of this long period of doubt, school administrators called us into an assembly to announce the solution that had been reached by the Indian Education Minister and the Office of His Holiness the Dalai Lama. Since there was not enough funding for everyone to continue his or her graduate studies, only fifteen students out of the forty in our class would continue to be supported. Those fifteen would be chosen by looking at the scores on the undergraduate final exams. We had heard rumors that everyone had passed their exams, but we had no idea where each of us ranked in the scoring. The assembly, which was attended by the whole student body, was shrouded in anxiety. No one dared to breathe until the names were called. Those who didn't make the top fifteen would not be able to continue their studies unless they could somehow support themselves, and for me it would certainly mean returning to my parents' home in South India for a life of hard labor.

One by one they called out the names in order of the top fifteen, and the identified students stood up. The ninth name that echoed through the assembly was mine, and I stood up full of relief and joy. I had studied extremely hard to prepare for the exams, but some of my classmates who I knew were more learned than I didn't make the top fifteen. These were people whom I had asked for help on certain subjects. I prayed they would be able to continue their education and find the means for their dreams and aspirations to be fulfilled.

Over the next three years I worked toward my acharya degree, the equivalent to a master's degree in the West. At this level there was much less focus on language study and more deep study of the most subtle aspects of Buddhist philosophy. We were expected to develop a profound understanding of the Buddhist science of the mind, which is at once both philosophy and psychology. In frequent all-night debates we would argue and defend the finest points and demonstrate our knowledge of the most important texts.

There were short debates with classmates almost every evening, but a few times a year there were more intense debates in which the whole student body of the Kagyu sect participated. Now we were studying the deeper and more complex texts of the Madhyamaka, the Middle Way school, including the texts of Nagarjuna and Chandrakirti. In these all-night debates, two acharya candidates were selected and seated on cushions facing the rest of the student body. There were teachers sitting to the side to moderate and evaluate the debaters' responses. I remember sitting there myself as one of the selected debaters, sweating profusely. The tea I was sipping didn't have much taste, and the room seemed extremely hot.

The two of us took turns answering questions put by our fellow students. Because we were ninth-year students, we were responsible for everything we had learned in those nine years! I remember that as we answered those questions, and as the night went on, the room got cooler and the tea seemed to taste better. In some ways this was a very serious event. We were demonstrating our knowledge and wisdom publicly to the whole Kagyu student body. I can't say I answered everything perfectly, but overall I would say that I performed above average.

There was another way by which we were expected to demonstrate our proficiency as senior students working toward our acharya degrees. In the evenings, after dinner, a gong would sound. All of the Kagyu students in the hostel would gather in the shrine room and chant. We would recite various root texts from the Tibetan Kagyu tradition, as well as texts from Indian masters such as Chandrakirti and Nagarjuna. Those students that were in their first six years and working toward their shastra degree would read from their own copies of the texts, and in this way would get extra practice for the exams of memorization. However, as senior students who had already completed that course of study and passed all of our exams, we were expected to be able to chant the texts exclusively from memory. Just one of these root texts could have as many as eight to ten chapters, or more.

Memorizing and debating form the core of the educational system in the East. By completely memorizing the root texts of our philosophical traditions, we construct the foundations of learning required to build deeper understandings and realizations of philosophy. It is the skillful use of that knowledge in argumentation and debate by which we demonstrate true depth of realization of the most profound teachings and our abilities to think critically about Buddhist philosophy.

PUBLISHING THE KANGYUR

After I had graduated and received my acharya degree, all of the Kagyu students were gathered in an assembly of the entire student body and were read a letter from His Holiness the Sixteenth Karmapa's General Secretary. The letter described a position open in one of the Karmapa's publishing projects—they needed a very learned editor. Without hesitation I raised my hand and accepted the position. I thought to myself, "I can't think of a better job than helping His Holiness through his publishing projects."

I traveled from Varanasi to Delhi to become chief managing editor for a project to publish the Kangyur, the entire collection of Buddha Shakya-muni's teachings. It was a good job with very good pay. I was living comfortably and, if truth be told, I couldn't have imagined an easier lifestyle. Many lamas were working on the actual transcriptions, and I was simply responsible for the final proofread: if I thought it was good, I would give it my stamp of approval. My new role brought not only good money but great respect. Many of my classmates from university would have considered it a dream job.

Yet somehow, even with this fortunate position, I was still unsatisfied. Delhi is the capital city of India and an international center of business and trade. It is busy with the comings and goings of people from all over the world, and I began to see that life there was full of distractions. I wondered what was the good of all the knowledge and wisdom I'd gained from academic study if, here in the bustling city, I was just as distracted as any other resident. I began to feel that it was time to practice in secluded retreat, and to experience for myself the realizations of dharma that come through intensive practice. I had dreams of the traditional three-year retreat.

I wrote letters to two retreat masters, Venerable Bokar Rinpoche and Venerable Khyentse Rinpoche, explaining my situation and asking if they would accept me in their retreats. I told myself I would focus on the one that responded first. I knew, in fact, that both retreats were under the guidance of the Very Venerable Kalu Rinpoche, so I had complete faith that either one would be blessed by his enlightened wisdom and activity. They both responded quickly, saying they would be happy to have someone with my level of education and experience enter their retreat. However, Khyentse Rinpoche's letter arrived first, so that is the invitation that I accepted.

At my job, I reported directly to His Holiness the Sixteenth Karmapa's publishing manager, Mr. Tsongpon Konchok. Now, I had to approach him to say that I wished to leave my position. At first I didn't explain I was going on retreat, and he got very angry. "What good is your degree," he asked me, "if you can't help the lineage?" He even offered to increase my salary to entice me to stay. I finally had to explain that money wasn't the problem, and that I wanted to enter retreat. However, he simply didn't believe me, and still wasn't prepared to grant me permission to leave. "Look," I said, "time will tell us who is right. If I do nothing but go straight into retreat, then I am right. If I go do something else, then you are right. Time will tell." He responded with silence, but finally let me go.

Years later, after I had completed retreat, I went to visit him, since he was my first boss who actually paid me a salary. Fortunately, there were no hard feelings lingering between us. He was happy to see me, and took me out to eat at a restaurant, where we chatted and laughed about it.

THREE-YEAR RETREAT: THE SACRED, SECRET, VAJRAYANA PRACTICE

I was about twenty-seven years old when I made the journey to the Venerable Khyentse Rinpoche's retreat center. On my way to enter retreat, I enjoyed some very happy and auspicious events. I was traveling from Delhi to India's Bihar Province, not too far from Bodhgaya. After the fifteen-hour train ride from Delhi, I arrived at the small city of Ambikapur. It would still be a couple of hours by bus from there to the Tibetan camp at Mainpat, where the retreat center is located. I learned I would have to wait until the next morning to complete that final leg of the trip. At the hotel, I met a friendly young couple who were also traveling to Mainpat in the morning. As we were getting along well, we looked forward to making the bus trip together. To me, it felt good to have some friendly traveling companions. When I spoke a little more about why I was headed to Mainpat, the young woman further delighted me by telling me that her father, the highly respected leader of the camp, had spoken of a young monk who was expected at the retreat. He was, of course, referring to me! Her father's name was King Namkhai Dorje, and I felt honored he had mentioned my arrival.

LAMA DUDJOM DORJEE IN RETREAT.
PHOTOGRAPH COURTESY OF THE AUTHOR.

As I arrived at Mainpat a large gathering of people was forming, and the manager of the monastery greeted me and took me into the kitchen for tea. As I sipped, he told me my arrival was fortunately timed, and I appeared to have auspicious connections. That said, he urged me to drink my tea quickly and proceed directly to the monastery shrine room. He explained that Venerable Khyentse Rinpoche had just returned from abroad and he was about to begin a longevity ceremony during which he would make special offerings. It seemed I was arriving at a very special time indeed.

Just as a monk escorted me into the shrine room, Venerable Khyentse Rinpoche was beginning the Mandala Offering Ceremony before a crowd of hundreds of monks and laypeople. As the ceremony ended, everyone welcomed me warmly. The local people exclaimed that "the new lama" must be a very special being to arrive at the precise moment of the longevity ceremony. Their words flattered me, though I did not believe I was such a special being. This was, however, an auspicious coincidence and a very joyous beginning to what would be the three most transformative years of my life.

In retreat, we concentrated all of our time and energy, without exception, on purifying our obscurations—on clearing away or cutting through whatever kept us from recognizing our true nature. There was intense meditation and study all day, and even at night we engaged in dream yoga practice; not a moment was wasted. A student once asked if, when I was in retreat, I was ever worried I wasn't getting enough sleep. My answer was, "On the contrary!" I was more worried about not wasting even a single minute of that precious opportunity for practice.

Retreat can certainly seem lonely from the outside. We spent nearly twenty-four hours a day in our retreat cabins. And even within the cabins, most of our time was spent inside our meditation box. The meditation box is basically four low walls that surround one's meditation cushion; the walls are only about a foot tall. The only people we saw were other retreatants and the cook, who was our only contact whatsoever with the outside world. Obviously there were no phones, televisions, restaurants, bills to pay, friends to gossip with, or leaky roofs to fix. With all of the ordinary distractions of mundane human existence almost completely eliminated, the only thing left to face was the greatest and, really, the only true obstacle: our own monkey minds.

Early in my retreat I experienced great difficulty. There was a very strict and structured schedule of group and individual practices, as well as many new texts and practices to learn. I struggled with my physical body a bit—my knees and legs hurt from sitting cross-legged so much. Eventually, though, my body adjusted and began to relax quite deeply. Once my body became accustomed to so much sitting and the worldly distractions faded away, retreat began to feel like a great rest after a long, tiring struggle.

The schedule we kept during the three-year retreat was far more rigorous than most people can even begin to imagine. We would formally begin our day around four a.m., and not finish until around ten p.m. Even when we finished our practices in the evening we did not go to bed, we simply stayed in our meditation box and did dream yoga until the next morning. At the very beginning of the retreat we did the Four Extraordinary Preliminary Practices, known as *ngondro*. The ngondro consists of four distinct sets of practices: one hundred thousand (actually 111,111) prostrations, and the same number each of Vajrasattva sadhana practice, mandala offering, and guru yoga practice. We completed ngondro within approximately six months, but I should mention that we were also doing other practices during that time. Over the course of three years, three months, and three days, we worked our way through extensive practice of all of the major sadhanas of the Kagyu lineage. We completed the lineage holders' guru yoga practices, such as Karma Pakshi, Gampopa, Milarepa, and Marpa. We also completed the sadhana practices of Vajrayogini, the Six Yogas of Naropa, Mahakala, Chakrasamvara, Hevajra, and others. We practiced Akshobhya and Vairochana sadhanas, as well as Prajnaparamita and Chöd. Of all of these, the Six Yogas of Naropa comprised the bulk of our practice during our years in retreat.

Though I hardly left my tiny retreat cabin, I had many wondrous experiences that a hundred journeys around the world could never have matched. Three-year retreat was like taking a lifetime's vacation away from samsara; I was able to have an extended amount of time removed from the day-to-day concerns of the mundane world. I was able to focus on spiritual practice to a degree that was indescribable. That alone, that peace, serenity, and tranquility produced by disentangling my experience of reality from the usual human pursuits of samsara, was enough to create some profound change in me. But beyond that, the intensive practices of the Vajrayana path also produced many profound results.

Away from the mundane world, my hair grew and grew, as perhaps did my wisdom and insight. This I do know: if I hadn't entered retreat I certainly wouldn't be the gentle, jolly person that people claim I am today. That intensive practice deepened my patience and purified my negative emotions in a way I never would have understood before retreat. Let me be quite clear: there are very few people left on this earth who could tell you tales of what I was like before entering retreat, but here I am not afraid to speak openly and honestly. Even before entering retreat, I was certainly a man of spirituality. As a small child I used to sit in meditation posture (although I did not really know what I was supposed to be doing with my mind as I sat there unmoving). I would mimic the activities of the lamas by attempting to say prayers to liberate any dead animals I happened to come across. When it was time to catch and kill livestock to feed our nomadic family, I would refuse to help and even run away until the butchering was finished because it offended my more compassionate side.

However, I was also a man deeply tainted by karma, samskaras, and kle-

His Holiness the Sixteenth Gyalwa Karmapa,
Rangjung Rigpe Dorje.
PHOTOGRAPHER UNKNOWN. COURTESY OF SHAMBHALA ARCHIVES.

shas. I was just as poisoned by passion, aggression, and ignorance as the rest of my fellow humans. As a young man I was terribly competitive and was known to have quite a hot temper. In order to come out on top, I was more than willing to steamroll my opponent, whether in a debate or a fistfight. During my time in retreat, working with the powerfully transformative yidam practices of the Kagyu lineage, there were times that I could see and feel with complete certainty that specific negative karmas were being dissolved. It was as though the less savory aspects of my personality were being put to the torch, as though I was being further refined by the fire of practice from crude ore into more purified gold. Although there is still much work to be done, I do feel as though I made some significant progress during that time in retreat, progress that could not have been matched by walking any other path.

One of the greatest benefits of secluded retreat was that I completed it with a deep sense of confidence and faith, not just in the buddha dharma but also in my own ability to create positive karma through practicing and teaching that dharma. When I entered retreat, I had some nagging doubts about how I was about to spend the next three years of my life. Of course I questioned how effective and productive the practices would be for me. As I continued through these intensive practices of the Vajrayana, however, my skepticism melted away, leaving me with a profound sense of certainty that I could not possibly be spending my time in a better way, and that I was being transformed into a better person, one who could truly contribute to helping himself and others to find the path to freedom, liberation from the sufferings of samsara.

You can judge the value of my three-year retreat for yourself: look at my involvement with the dharma during the past three decades. My helping to grow various dharma centers in the West, the teachings I have given, the students who follow me and the books and other media that I've produced testify to the value of my retreat. I owe every accomplishment to my precious teachers and all other sentient beings. If I had not completed the traditional retreat, I definitely would have lived a very different life, and it certainly would not have been one of such rigorous commitment to spreading the teachings of the buddha dharma. It is thanks to my experience of retreat that you now hold this book in your hands.

Sarva mangalam!

The Story of Yolmo Kangra

O N THE BORDER of Tibet and Nepal there is a place called Yolmo located in high snow mountains. It is a sacred place for the Kagyu Buddhist school because the great yogi Milarepa meditated in this mountain.

Particular caves are being discovered in which Milarepa meditated for many years. The local people call these tiger caves because mountain lions and tigers live in them. This place is also well recognized from the original text of the autobiography of Milarepa, called the *Hundred Thousand Songs of Milarepa.*

For most of the year the surrounding mountains are covered with snow. In order to get to this holy cave one must walk for at least a week from Kathmandu over untamed treacherous mountains and ferocious rivers.

Only a small handful of fortunate pilgrims have ever made it to this cave. Buddhists believe that to meditate at the cave of a great yogi such as Milarepa is an achievement of a lifetime.

I was part of a small group of people who took a helicopter and landed on the top of this mountain. As soon as we landed we felt a very special energy; on the way down, not only did we find the cave, we also found many small retreat cabins.

We were very fortunate that we had the Vajra Master Khenpo Tsultrim Gyamtso Rinpoche with us. Over a ten-day period we meditated alone in these cabins and also received daily spontaneous teachings from Rinpoche.

I felt this to be one of the highlights of my life, and infinitely beneficial to my meditation experience. I felt my devotion and confidence increase a little bit every day. One morning during this retreat I woke up and, as I meditated, I had some special experiences. Immediately I grabbed a pen and wrote down some of my experiences in the form of a *doha,* a spontaneous poem of realization, which you will find below. I wrote the rough draft in Tibetan and then gave it to Rinpoche. One month later Rinpoche gave me

LAMA DUDJOM DORJEE.

PHOTOGRAPH BY SARITE SANDERS.

COURTESY OF KARMA TRIYANA DHARMACHAKRA.

the poem back, except this time it included an English translation by one of his professional translators. Because Rinpoche had taken the poem and invested his own time and energy having it translated, I took this to mean that there was some value in the words of this doha, especially now that Rinpoche himself had become involved.

Because of all this it is available for you to read now. Because it comes from Rinpoche I am hoping it carries some type of blessings, and will help to establish and deepen your connection to Rinpoche and the lineage of shamatha, vipashyana, and Mahamudra.

PRAISE TO YOLMO KANGRA BY LAMA DUDJOM DORJEE.

CALLIGRAPHY BY LAMA DUDJOM DORJEE.

PRAISE TO YOLMO KANGRA
by Lama Dudjom Dorjee

This place of Yolmo Kangra
Was clearly foretold of in the *Avatamsaka Sutra*.
The Lord of Yogis, Jetsun Milarepa,
Went through hardships in twenty fortresses.
This Great Fortress of Tiger Cave and Lion
Is surely one of the secret fortresses.
It is also well known as the Guru's hidden place.
The good qualities of the fortress are inconceivable!
Oh, how this fortress can be praised!
Up there, in the turquoise-colored sky,
Are clouds as white as the white of the snow-mountains' white
Down here on the hills forested with wish-fulfilling trees,
I enjoy the melodious songs of all the birds
With ornaments of snow mountain tormas in the background.
Way down, the voice of the river's sound
Resounds continuously as self-arisen mantra.
The wind blowing from mountain to mountain
Plays the self-arisen sound of conch shell music.
I, the mountain son, staying in this place
Have the good fortune to grow in experience and realization.

This was spoken by Lama Dudjom Dorje while staying in retreat.

Acknowledgments

THERE ARE A few individuals without whom this text never would have come into existence. Thanks to their efforts, the dharma wheel continues this particular turning.

I wish to thank these people for helping to bring this project to completion for the benefit of all sentient beings:

Aaron Price, for the initial assistance with translation, editing, and original writing, as well as organization and design.

Sherry Jaco, for artistic direction and graphic design, as well as formatting and layout.

Maureen Peters, for her assistance in writing the section on the Twelve Deeds of the Buddha.

Linda Sperling, for glossary construction, indexing, and final editing of a quality that most writers could never even dream of.

Beth Keenan, for tirelessly working to maintain my web presence, so that my dharma activity has a national and even international reach. Thanks to her, this book, like so much other work that I have done, will be disseminated far and wide for the benefit of so many more beings.

John Springer and Derek Meyers, for finding the right definition for dharma terms as well as conventional terms to choose the appropriate terminology during the process of writing the book.

Finally, I would like to express my gratitude to Tashi Chotso and Tashi Dolkar for both their patience and continuous support during the creation and final fruition of this book, my latest turning of the dharma wheel.

Lama Dudjom Dorjee
Sarva mangalam!

Glossary

Akshobhya (Sanskrit: "The Immovable One"). One of the Five Wisdom Buddhas, lord of the eastern pure land.

arhat (Sanskrit: "the perfected one"). One who has attained nirvana.

bardo (Tibetan: "in-between state"). In the Vajrayana, six in-between states are defined: the bardo of birth, the dream bardo, the bardo of meditation, bardo of the moment of death, the bardo of ultimate reality, and the bardo of becoming (rebirth).

bhumi (Sanskrit: "land"). Term for the ten stages through which a bodhisattva must pass to attain buddhahood.

bindu (Sanskrit: "point" or "dot"). Translated into Tibetan as *tigle,* or "drop"; an aspect of the subtle body of the human energy system.

bodhichitta (Sanskrit: "enlightenment mind"). In Mahayana and Vajrayana, the attitude of enlightenment, the "heart of awakening" to loving-kindness and compassion for other beings, which is the prelude to becoming a bodhisattva.

bodhisattva (Sanskrit: "enlightenment existence"). A "buddha in training," i.e., a being who generates enormous compassion and works tirelessly for the benefit of all sentient beings.

buddha (Sanskrit: "awakened one"). A being in a state of perfect enlightenment, embodying all virtues and thus able to help countless beings. Historically, Siddhartha Gautama Shakyamuni, supreme teacher, is the buddha of our age.

Chakrasamvara (Sanskrit: "Wheel of Supreme Bliss"). Associated with the highest yoga tantra of Vajrayana Buddhism, this *yidam,* or meditational deity, typically appears in *yab-yum* (sexual union) with his consort, Vajravarahi, demonstrating the inseparable union of wisdom and compassion.

Chöd (Tibetan: "Severing"). A Vajrayana spiritual practice designed to cut through the ego and sever the illusion of a separate self, introduced by the great female yogini Machig Labdrön.

Gampopa (1079–1153). "The Physician from Dagpo" studied under Milarepa and later numbered the First Karmapa, Dusum Khyenpa, among his many disciples. Renowned for his *Jewel Ornament of Liberation,* unifying the teachings of Atisha and Tilopa.

gyalpo (Tibetan: "king"). In the legends of the Tibetan people, spirits who may either be malevolent or bound by oath to be protectors.

Hevajra (Sanskrit: "Indestructible"). One of the most important tantric *yidams* (meditational deities), associated with the rooting out of all unskillful actions. His principal practice text is known as the *Hevajra Tantra.*

Hinayana (Sanskrit: "Poorer" or "Lesser [Spiritual] Vehicle"), a term pejoratively used by Mahayanists, to describe the first and oldest foundation of Buddhist practice, focusing on personal salvation from the three poisons, achieving samadhi, and arhatship.

Kagyu (Tibetan: "Oral Transmission [Lineage]"). One of the six main schools of Tibetan Buddhism, tracing descent from Tilopa, Naropa, Marpa, Milarepa, and Gampopa; also known as the "Whispered Lineage" for its profound emphasis on guru yoga.

Kangyur (Tibetan: "The Word[s]"). Tibetan collection of sacred texts in about 108 volumes presumed to have been the words spoken by the Buddha himself. Most likely, all of these texts once had Sanskrit originals, although some are translated from other languages.

Karmapa (Tibetan: "Buddhist Activity Embodiment"). The Gyalwang Karmapa is the spiritual head of the largest segment of the Kagyu lineage.

The Karmapas have incarnated in *nirmanakaya* form (manifestation bodies) for seventeen lifetimes to the present day.

Karma Pakshi. The second Gyalwang Karmapa (1203–1283), advisor to Kublai Khan, famously revered for introducing the melodic chant of the six-syllable mantra, OM MANI PEME HUM, and for composing one hundred texts.

kleshas (Sanskrit: "defilements" or "afflictive emotions"). Unwholesome mental states resulting from the three poisons, which can manifest as negative actions.

Mahamudra (Sanskrit: the "Great Symbol" or "Great Seal"). The deepest meditation on the nature of all phenomena. Mahamudra is beyond concept, projection, and imagination; it is the "sealed" union of wisdom and emptiness.

Mahaparinirvana (Sanskrit: "Great Going Beyond into Nirvana"). Shakyamuni Buddha's final passing into the nonreturning, deathless state at age eighty.

mahasiddha (Sanskrit: "great master of perfections"). A being who has achieved perfect individual realization and has thereby attained visible signs of having many blessings and unusual abilities.

Mahayana (Sanskrit: "Greater [Spiritual] Vehicle"). Larger of the two major traditions of Buddhism (Theravada being the other), includes the Vajrayana. Its focus is upon achieving complete enlightenment for the benefit of all sentient beings.

Manjushri (Sanskrit: "Gentle Glory"). The bodhisattva of transcendent wisdom, closely associated with the Prajnaparamita sutras. He is typically shown seated, wielding a flaming sword with his right arm and, with his left hand, holding a lotus which supports a text.

Mantrayana (Sanskrit: "Sacred Utterance Vehicle"). Tantric Buddhism, widely synonymous with Vajrayana.

mara (Sanskrit: "destroyer" or "demon"). A collective term for anything that obstructs enlightenment; most often presented as being of four types: internal, i.e., craving; mental afflictions; the five skandhas, or aggregates (forms, sensations, perceptions, thoughts, and consciousness); and death itself.

Marpa Lotsawa (Tibetan: "Marpa the Translator," 1012–1097). The first person to bring and translate the precious teachings of Tilopa and Naropa from India, thereby founding the Kagyu lineage in Tibet. He was also famously the guru of Milarepa.

merit (Sanskrit: *punya*). A concept in Buddhism that posits accumulating good actions and thoughts which carry over to the next life and can contribute to our future liberation.

Milarepa (Tibetan: "Mila the Cotton-Clad," ca. 1052–1135). Tibet's most famous yogi and poet, who with superhuman effort achieved liberation in one lifetime. He is celebrated for composing some 100,000 spontaneous *dohas,* or songs, teaching the most subtle points of Mahamudra.

mudra (Sanskrit: "seal," "mark," or "gesture"). Symbolic or ritual motion of the hands which helps the flow of prana through the channels when meditating.

nadis (Sanskrit: "channels"). The complex network through which prana flows.

nagas (Sanskrit: "serpents"). Mythological beings, half serpent and half human, believed to control waters, lakes, seas, and rain. The naga king is said to have sheltered Shakyamuni Buddha from rain as he meditated under the bodhi tree.

nirvana (Sanskrit: "blowing out," "extinction"). That state of transcendence wherein there is no suffering, no desire, and no illusions of self. A being in nirvana is permanently liberated from the effects of karma and the repetition of bodily existence.

parinirvana (Sanskrit: "after or beyond extinction"). Refers to death of the body of one who has attained complete awakening into buddhahood.

Prajnaparamita (Sanskrit: "Perfection of Transcendent Wisdom"). Combining the words for *prajna* (wisdom) with *paramita* (perfect virtue), *Prajnaparamita* refers to both a collection of sutras and an essential Buddhist concept, i.e., the realization that all phenomena are illusory.

prana (Sanskrit: "life force" or "vital principle"). The energy that flows through the body and is most perceptible as breath.

sadhana (Sanskrit: "means of accomplishment"). Both the discipline of spiritual practice itself and the ritual texts utilized for practicing.

samadhi (Sanskrit: "establish," "to make firm"). Deep meditative absorption, where the mind is firmly concentrated and still in one-pointed meditation.

Samantabhadra (Sanskrit: "Universal Worth"). A great bodhisattva in the Mahayana teachings who is considered, especially in the Nyingma lineage of Vajrayana, as a primordial buddha. He is celebrated as the wellspring of generosity, and aspirations are made to emulate his boundless offerings.

samsara (Sanskrit: "to flow on"). Endless births, lives, deaths, and rebirths in the six realms of existence—the hells, the hungry ghost realm, the animal kingdom, the human sphere, the jealous god realms, and the god realms—through which beings cycle until attaining realization.

samskara (Sanskrit: "that which has been put together"). Used to designate "mental formation" or psychological conditioning that gives rise to future volitional actions.

shamatha (Sanskrit: "calmness, "tranquility"). Mind stabilizing, calm abiding, tranquility meditation.

siddhi (Sanskrit: "perfection," "accomplishment," or "attainment"). Complete, enlightened understanding attained by a master yogi; also sometimes miraculous spiritual powers possessed by a *siddha* (great sage).

sutra (Sanskrit: "thread"). Any text traditionally regarded as the words of Shakyamuni Buddha.

thangka (Tibetan: "rendering"). A painting on cloth depicting *yidams* or a mandala as a visual support for meditation.

three jewels. Objects of refuge for all Buddhists: the Buddha (who gave the teachings), the dharma (the teachings themselves), and the sangha (the lamas, monks, and nuns who preserve and perpetuate the Buddha's teachings). The three jewels are the first and outer source of refuge.

three poisons. Ignorance; desire and its concomitant attachment; aversion and its manifestation, anger: the potent obstacles to be overcome in our quest for enlightenment.

three roots. The lama (guru); the yidam (meditational deity); and the protectors (dharmapalas, dakas, and dakinis), forming the second or inner of the three sources of refuge. The third and secret refuge is the *Trikaya*, or Three Bodies of the Buddha.

Vairochana (Sanskrit: "Illuminator"). The Supreme Buddha, the embodiment of emptiness. Vairochana is also one of the Five Wisdom Buddhas; his is the central pure land.

vajra (Sanskrit: "thunderbolt" and "diamond"). Represents firmness of spiritual power; also an implement used in tantric practice to symbolize emptiness.

Vajrayana (Sanskrit: "Thunderbolt Way" or "Diamond Way"). One of the three major branches of Buddhism; its methods employ intricate ritual and focus on direct initiation from a qualified guru.

vipashyana (Sanskrit: "insight"). As distinguished from shamatha meditation, vipashyana investigates the nature of the mind and of reality.